THE WAVERLEY ROUTE

THROUGH TIME

Roy G. Perkins

With Iain MacIntosh

AMBERLEY

Preface

The reader is asked to note that where possible equivalent contemporary views to the historic photographs have been provided, though that has not been feasible because of tree growth, new buildings or level changes in some cases. Such cases have been noted in the script. We apologise for such examples but a visit to the sites involved will illustrate the difficulties.

Roy G. Perkins
Iain MacIntosh

Front Cover
Top: A north-bound stopping service stands in the platform at Newcastleton behind V2 60816 as an unidentified locomotive, believed to be an A2, drifts south off the climb to Whitrope with a Niddrie Yard to Carlisle Canal Yard freight in the summer of 1962.

Bottom: Today, the location is the Lidalia caravan site and has changed beyond recognition. The former loading dock and the base of the goods shed are still evident within the site though. The location of the goods yard throat is now a storage area for caravans, as can be seen.

Back Cover
Top: The scene of the closure protests lead by the Reverend Mabern was Newcastleton level crossing. A group had gathered and stopped the passage of the Night Midlander for more than two hours before peace could be restored and the train allowed on its way.

Bottom: In 2012, only a slight rise in the road and a pile of stone indicates that this was the location of Newcastleton level crossing and station. The station master's house still stands to the left of the scene.

First published 2012

Amberley Publishing
The Hill, Stroud, Gloucestershire, GL5 4EP
www.amberley-books.com

Copyright © Roy G. Perkins and Iain MacIntosh, 2012

The right of Roy G. Perkins and Iain MacIntosh to be identified as the Authors of this work has been asserted in accordance with the Copyrights, Designs and Patents Act 1988.

ISBN 978 1 4456 0960 7

British Library Cataloguing in Publication Data.
A catalogue record for this book is available from the British Library.

Typesetting by Amberley Publishing.

Printed in Great Britain.

Introduction

The origins of the Waverley Route can be best explained by reference to the development of Edinburgh and its growing appetite for coal; it wasn't known as 'Auld Reekie' for nothing. First on the scene, authorised in 1826 and opened in 1831, was the Edinburgh & Dalkeith Railway (the 'Innocent Railway') which was an independent company operating the railway by a mixture of horses and stationary engines despite having powers to use locomotives. Constructed to the 'Scotch Gauge' of 4 feet 6 inches, it was primarily constructed for the haulage of coal from the Lothian coalfield to its terminus at Edinburgh, St Leonards, which it reached via one of the world's first railway tunnels, which achieved a length of 572 yards and was lit by gas lamps, with the trains hauled up the 1 in 30 gradients by cable from a stationary engine at St Leonards. In 1834 an extension to Fisherrow Harbour at Musselburgh was opened and in 1835 a further extension to the port of Leith came into operation. In common with many other early Scottish railways, it retained its distinctive 4 feet 6 inch gauge until it was absorbed by a larger company and subsumed into the national network. In the case of the Edinburgh & Dalkeith this occurred in October 1845 when it was bought by the North British Railway for £113,000. The southern extension of this railway from South Esk, a.k.a. Dalhousie, toward Arniston Engine was undertaken by the Marquis of Lothian's Waggonway and involved, at its northern extremity, the construction of a very substantial viaduct variously known as Newtongrange Viaduct or Newbattle Viaduct. A the southern end of this viaduct, in an area known as Newtongrange, a substantial community was to grow-up which eventually reached such proportions as to warrant its own railway station, Newtongrange, which opened on 1 January 1908. Much of the success of the Newtongrange conurbation was as a result of the development of Lady Victoria Pit and similar local mining activities. The Pit is now closed but its site is home to the Scottish Mining Museum and as such is something of a tourist attraction in its own right.

To return to our chronology, however, in 1844 the incorporation of the North British Railway on 19 July had significant ramifications not only for the Edinburgh & Dalkeith Railway but for the railway history of the whole of Scotland. This company was authorised with a capital of £800,000 and powers to borrow a further £266,666 and invested with the powers to build a line from Edinburgh to Berwick-upon-Tweed, where it formed an end-on junction with the York, Newcastle & Berwick Railway. In addition, it was by its Act enabled to build a branch line from Longniddry to Haddington. As has been seen already, the North British Railway purchased the Edinburgh & Dalkeith Railway in 1845, thereby signalling the imperialist nature of the company, which was further confirmed by its acquisition of the Edinburgh & Hawick Railway in 1846.

The immediate effect of the purchase of the Edinburgh & Dalkeith Railway by the North British was closure, but unlike many later closures this was closure to some purpose. The North British had opted to adopt the United Kingdom standard gauge of 4 feet 8½ inches whereas the Edinburgh & Dalkeith had built to the 'Scotch Gauge' of 4 feet 6 inches. The North British resolved to rebuild the Dalkeith enterprise to its own standard and for this and other works it was necessary to close the railway. When it re-opened in 1847 it was on a slightly different alignment, a slightly different gauge and, perhaps most significantly of all, it was worked by locomotive engines. The horses and cable haulage had gone, never to return. The stage was thus set for the North British's next foray into railway construction – the advance on Hawick.

As part of the reconstruction works on the Edinburgh & Dalkeith, a new viaduct had been built across the River South Esk near South Esk or Dalhousie station. Eskbank station had a particular significance because it became the interchange station for the Peebles loop, though the physical junction was at Hardengreen. This Peebles loop, opened in July 1855, was initially served by the fiercely independent Peebles Railway until that company was finally taken over by the North British in 1876. We shall return to the Peebles Railway later in this introduction. This was now utilised to cross the river and aim for the next main objective of the railway: Galashiels. However, long before this the substantial barrier of the Lammermuir Hills had to be negotiated. The reader should perhaps at this point be reminded that virtually everything that was built, hewn, erected, dug or moved had to be tackled by hand. The main exception was solid rock, which was often blasted before being carried, lifted or moved by hand to its next resting place. In a few cases, temporary waggonways were built to move spoil from cuttings, for example to the site of major embankment works. It was hard physical work carried on, in the main, regardless of the weather, under conditions which would make most of today's workforce weep. Through Gorebridge, opened in early July 1847, they toiled, on to Fushiebridge, opened on the same day as its near neighbour. From the start of the railway in Edinburgh, they had been climbing; now the terrain had changed and they were out onto the exposed hills as they started the climb up through Borthwick to Tynehead Station, which was opened on 4 August 1848. Over Falahill they continued; then began the tortuous journey down Gala Water, crossing and re-crossing that river, through Heriot, opened on 4 August 1848, and on to Fountainhall Station, which was later to become the junction for the Lauder Light Railway. Further down the valley, Stow was opened on the same day, as was Bowland, while the important objective of Galashiels was not finally reached until 20 January 1849, well over a year after they had started. Over the ensuing years Galashiels was to become an important junction, from where lines radiated first to Selkirk (opened on 5 April 1856) and then to Peebles via Innerleithen (opened 18 June 1866).The North British regarded Peebles as part of its railway fiefdom in the Borders. The authorisation of the Symington, Bigger, & Broughton in May 1858 was a set-back to its plans for a railway monopoly in the Central Borders because it potentially allowed direct access from the Caledonian main line at Symington to Peebles and thence into the Borders. As might be expected, the North British retaliated with a proposal to build a railway from Galashiels to Peebles via Innerleithen, effectively blocking any further eastward progress by the Caledonian. Thus Peebles became the eastern extremity of the Caledonian Railway, at least in the Borders.

The railway forged on toward Hawick, with the important town and tourist destination of Melrose reached in February 1849 and the remaining line right through to Hawick opening on 1 November 1849. This last section included a short-lived station at Newstead: the important station of St Boswells, which later became the junction for lines to Duns and Berwick as well as those to Jedburgh, Kelso and Berwick. After St Boswells there were intermediate stations at Belses and Hassendean before Hawick itself was reached on 1 November 1849. It appears that Hassendean Station was not however opened until somewhat later than the rest; in fact, its first appearance in the railway timetable was in March 1850.

There were usually great celebrations in towns when the railway arrived, bringing the prospect of increased prosperity to the communities involved. In the case of Hawick, however, such celebrations were decidedly muted because the town was in the grip of another cholera epidemic.

If the North British Railway had had something of a skirmish with the rival Caledonian Railway over access to Peebles, full-scale war broke out between the two in the 1850s. The Caledonian had of course already secured access to the great Border city of Carlisle in September 1847 with its line from Carstairs but the North British was resolved not to be outdone and as early as 1845 secured the services of the famous Scottish railway engineer John Miller to survey a line from Hawick to Carlisle via Langholm. This scheme was never proceeded with.

Proposals and counter proposals from the two sides were aired through a series of public meetings throughout the Border towns and villages as well as at the Palace of Westminster and the language used at these meetings was at times vitriolic, to say the least. Finally, in 1859, the North British won the day with a plan to build a line from Hawick to Carlisle via Liddesdale which by-passed the town of Langholm completely, though it did provided it with a branch line. The significance of this change of route does not appear to have been particularly obvious to the populace of the day. Looking from today's perspective, it seems to have centered on the figure of J. F. Tone. Tone was the engineer of the nearby Border Counties Railway and early in the 1850s he took ownership of the coal workings at Plashetts in the North Tyne Valley. At the time these coal workings were seen as potentially very important, not least to the Border Counties Railway. While they were ostensibly friendly, the North British Railway and the North Eastern Railway were locked into a rivalry in which the North Eastern sought to protect its heartland around Newcastle and refused to allow the North British running powers into Newcastle itself. The North British devised a plan through its Chairman, Richard Hodgson, to gain its own independent access to Newcastle via the Border Counties Railway, the Wansbeck Railway and the Blythe & Tyne Railway and hence into the Blythe & Tyne's New Bridge Street Station. In fact, this plan was never put to the test and the North British Railway gained running powers from Hexham into Newcastle Central Station for its Border Counties trains. As a result, Reedsmouth Junction on the Border Counties and Wansbeck railways was relocated and re-configured to provide a south-facing junction rather than a north-facing one as originally envisaged.

Meanwhile, back in Hawick and following the approval by Parliament of plans for the Border Union Railway on 21 July 1859, plans were afoot for the start of construction. The building of the main line of railway was let as eight separate contracts, while the branch lines (Gretna, Langholm, Canonbie Colliery and the Border Counties) were subject to separate contracts. The first sod was cut at Hardie's Hill, opposite Lynwood House, on 7 September 1859 by the wife of Richard Hodgson, the NBR chairman, in the presence of many local and national dignitaries and to the strains of the band of the 16th Lancers. Progress was not as rapid as hoped. In Hawick itself, the existing station had largely to be abandoned and re-located to the south-east; then the River Teviot had to be crossed before the railway could weave its way between the streets of the town and out toward Hardie's Hill once more. Here, a further obstacle had to be overcome in the form of yet another viaduct, this time over Slitrig Water, and variously known as Slitrig or Lynwood Viaduct. Now, on the western side of Slitrig Water, the formation passed Stobs Castle, the ancestral seat of the Elliot family. This was a large estate some two miles south of Hawick, a substantial part of which was put up for sale in the early years of the twentieth century. The government showed an interest as the terrain was considered ideal for military training and thus was born Stobs Camp. The camp was adjacent to the farmhouse of Acreknowe and in time provided accommodation for some 4,500 men as well as its own hospital. In the vicinity of Acreknowe some significant sidings were provided for shunting and accommodating troop trains, controlled by a substantial signal box which was opened in 1903. In addition there was a narrow gauge railway from an interchange platform at Acreknowe to the hospital some distance away, powered by horses only. The railway forged on, however, climbing all the way before reaching the first of the original stations at Barns shortly after crossing a further viaduct of that same name. The station opened with the name Barns on 1 July 1862. It retained the name Barns only briefly, however, as it was renamed Stobs, after the Castle of Stobs, in September 1862. Still climbing, the railway next encountered the valley of the Langside Burn near Penchrise, which it crossed on the magnificent Shankend Viaduct. This viaduct, at 199 yards in length and containing fifteen masonry spans, was substantially renovated in 2007, with a new waterproof membrane added. It is now a Grade II listed building.

Immediately to the south of the viaduct stands Shankend Station, a small local station aimed at local agricultural produce which, despite its isolated situation and spartan passenger traffic, survived until the closure of the entire line in 1969. The station buildings at Shankend are extremely distinctive and nothing even vaguely similar is to be found elsewhere on the route. Still climbing and weaving its way through the hills, the railway's next objective is Whitrope Tunnel. This tunnel, at 1,208 yards in length, is noted for its imposing entrances, with that at the southern end the better known. Here there was also a short spur off the mainline and a trailing cross-over to facilitate the accommodation of pilot locomotives, which had been used, especially in the days of steam haulage, to assist the heavy trains up the gradients from Hawick and Newcastleton. The site of Whitrope siding is now home to the Waverley Route Heritage Association, who have established a heritage centre there, and to the Border Union Railway Company Limited, which operates a short length of heritage railway in the direction of Riccarton Junction.

Riccarton Junction was the next station on the railway's descent toward Newcastleton. This station was originally an important railway hub which provided railway access to Hexham, Newcastle and Morpeth as well as to the coal workings at Plashetts and the market town of Bellingham. In the early days the North British Railway had high hopes for Riccarton, providing as it did the route to Carlisle in one direction and to Newcastle in the other. In fact, its route to Newcastle by way of the Border Counties line provided a shorter route from Edinburgh to Newcastle than did the alternative route via Drem and Berwick.

In keeping with its hoped-for status as a major railway junction, Riccarton was provided with the largest engine shed between Edinburgh and Carlisle, a carriage shed, two coal loading stages, a turntable, a foundry and a large array of sidings, in addition to its own gas works.

Before the railway was built there was no centre of population at Riccarton, not even a clachan, so the railway built its own village to house its own staff. There was a row of semi-detached houses running up the side of Saughtree Fell and eventually two rows of terraced houses running along the flank of the same hill; a substantial house for the Station Master, standing in its own gardens; a school and school-house; and a final cottage attached to the south signal box. At its peak the population of the village reached some 180 people, most of them employed on the railway. The name of Riccarton is writ large in railway circles for it was a railway village which for many years had no road access; even the doctor had to come by train. Eventually, in 1956, with the closure of the Border Counties line it became possible, with permission, to drive a car into Riccarton but by then the significance of Riccarton was largely gone.

The next stopping point as the railway continues its tortuous descent was another isolated village at Steele-Road, as it was originally titled. Originally established as another railway settlement, Steele-Road was a clachan of no more than a dozen houses which boasted its own blacksmith's forge. But it had a road and a small railway station with a couple of sidings accessed by setting back off the main line. Indeed, at one stage it was a road-rail interchange point because after the Border Counties Railway closed in 1956 there was, briefly, a bus service from here down into the North Tyne Valley. At some time around the First World War the name was simplified to Steel Road.

Resuming our south-bound progress, the next stop was Newcastleton, which also marked the end of the long climb to Whitrope; with a population of about 1,000, this was the only population centre of any size between Hawick and Longtown on the outskirts of Carlisle, some 36 miles away.

Newcastleton was a fairly large station, with its two platforms; a long refuge siding at the south end of the station; a short refuge siding behind the down platform, historically used as a refuge for the Whitrope pilot; and an extensive goods yard with livestock pens, goods yard, goods shed and coal sidings and loading banks. Being at the foot of the climb to Whitrope summit, Newcastleton was operationally quite important too, particularly in the days of steam, when pilots (or banking engines) were attached here to the rear of trains which it was felt would not cope with the fearsome gradient unaided.

The next station after Newcastleton was Kershopefoot, hard up against the Anglo-Scottish border, which ran down the centre of Kershope Burn. Kershopefoot itself was, and remains, a small hamlet which happened to have/have had a railway station. The station was a small affair, with two sidings to accommodate a coal-yard and lime depot, a station building which also accommodated the Post Office and, originally on the up platform, the signal box. During the First World War this signal box was replaced by a taller and more substantial building at the northern end of the down platform. This building also accommodated the winding gear for the level crossing which had been recently installed. This crossing had been necessitated by the construction of a bridge over the River Liddell which replaced the previous ford. This in turn meant the end of the bridge under the station platforms which had previously served the ford. Passengers now crossed the line by means of the level crossing.

In early timetables a station is recorded at Nooks Pasture and for a long time this has baffled railway and local historians alike. There were never any buildings there, nor were there any goods facilities, and it appears this was more of a stopping place rather than a station. Nearby is the farmhouse of Nook and in the middle of the nineteenth century this was owned and occupied by Mr John Foster. Foster was a local landowner and a major shareholder in the Border Union Railway and it seems very likely that he used his position to arrange for trains to stop close to his residence of Nook. Certainly the rather more ornate style of the bridges on his land (239, 240 and 241) suggests that these too were dictated by him.

From Nook Pasture we progress south to Penton. This was another station with no obvious settlement to serve, for there was never a village of Penton. However, this was an area of good farming land and there were thus innumerable substantial farms nearby. In early days there was also a mill for corn nearby and substantial lime-works to the north of the station itself. There was one nearby farm which produced Guernsey milk and for that reason the morning Edinburgh to London express made an unadvertised stop here daily to collect this milk and speed it on its way.

The milk was too rich for local tastes but apparently suited London tastes rather better, for this practice continued almost to the end of services in 1969. Penton boasted two platforms, a goods yard with a central engine release road, and a coal siding at the southern end of the up platform, in addition to a large station house. A signal box was provided here as well and closed in February 1968.

Next station was Riddings (a.k.a. Riddings Junction, Canonbie Junction, Langholm Point Road, etc.). Riddings was where trains for Langholm left the main line on their short trip via Canonbie, Gilnockie and Tarras to Langholm. There was no village of Riddings, though the little hamlet of Moat was not far away. Riddings was built as and remained an exchange station, built for the convenience of passengers changing trains to and from Langholm. It was equipped with sidings, a loading bank, a signal box and a number of station buildings. There were also a number of cottages built for railway employees. It was equipped with three platforms, one of which served the Langholm branch, and a central engine release road, as at Penton.

To the south was the large Moat Quarry, with its extensive sidings, and then we come to the next station of Scotch Dyke (a.k.a. Scotsdike). Scotch Dyke stood on one of the few straight stretches of line on the southern part of the route and was equipped with refuge sidings and a goods yard with a loading bank and a level crossing to serve the unmade road to the clachan of Kirkandrews on Esk. Scotch Dyke was the northern terminus of the Waverley Route for a few months from at least 29 October 1861 to 1 March 1862, when the line to Newcastleton opened. In spite of this it was an early closure casualty in May 1949. The original signal box was also re-located from the southern end of the station to the northern end, adjacent to the level crossing. The station building, with its distinctive canopy motto, is still extant.

Longtown was the next station and for once boasted a substantial population. This station was also a junction, for it was here that the short-lived line to Gretna diverged. Its junction status and substantial population dictated the size of the station and accordingly there were originally engine sheds, a goods shed, loading banks, a coal yard and at one time no less than three signal boxes in addition to the substantial station house, similar to Penton and Lyneside. In very early days the North British ran through trains from Langholm to Gretna, though these didn't last long. Indeed, the Gretna branch itself didn't last long and was closed in August 1915 to all traffic, though it was re-opened to freight in 1923 after public pressure before being closed again in 1951. To what extent the termination of passenger trains to Gretna was dictated by the government, who had built a substantial armaments factory at Longtown and beyond, remains a mystery at the time of writing.

Lyneside was the next station southbound, though when it was first opened in 1861 it was titled West Linton after the nearby village. It was re-named Lineside in June 1870 and re-named again as Lyneside in December of the same year, which name it retained until it was closed to passengers in 1929. It boasted a substantial station house, a southbound refuge siding and a loop for coal traffic as well as a signal box.

Finally we come to Harker; first opened in 1861, it was never a popular station and accordingly was an early casualty, closing in 1929. During the Second World War the station was rebuilt with longer platforms at a slightly different location and in this guise lasted until the line closed in 1969. As built, it boasted a substantial southbound refuge siding and a loop for coal traffic as well as a signal box. The station building was single-storey, in marked difference to those at nearby Lyneside.

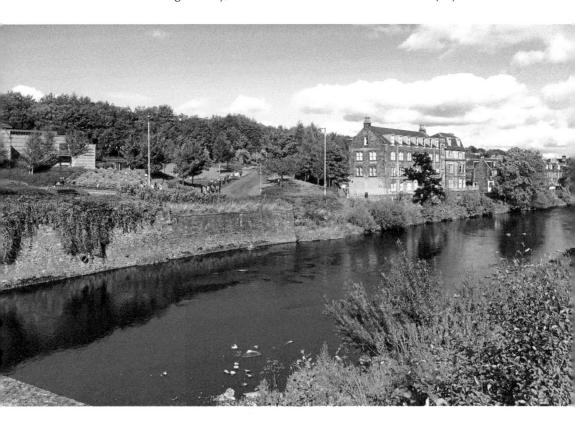

The Teviot flows gently through Hawick on its way to the Tweed and the North Sea at Berwick. The Teviotdale Leisure Centre stands to the top left, occupying the former station forecourt and yard. Until 1975 Teviot Viaduct, with the station platforms atop, had curved its way round, turning the route almost through 90 degrees to lift the line out of the town and into the Slitrig Valley beyond.

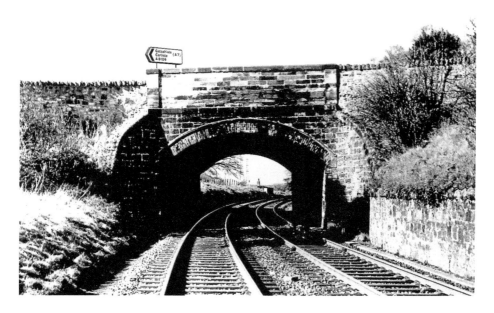

Bridge 11 at Sheriffhall in 1969. This bridge carried the A68 Edinburgh–Jedburgh road over the Waverley line just over 7 miles out from Waverley Station. South-bound trains had already been climbing for 2 miles at this point, 1¼ miles for freight departing Millerhill Yard. The climb to Falahill was continuous, with the exception of a short level section at Gorebridge, on varying gradients up to 1:70. This represented a serious start to journeys south and a stern test to footplate crews, especially in the days of steam.

A footpath was constructed in the mid-1990s on this section of line from Hardengreen to Sheriffhall and can be seen leaving the formation on the north side of the bridge in this 2005 shot. With the coming of the new Borders Railway, this footpath is to be rerouted with various options currently being considered.

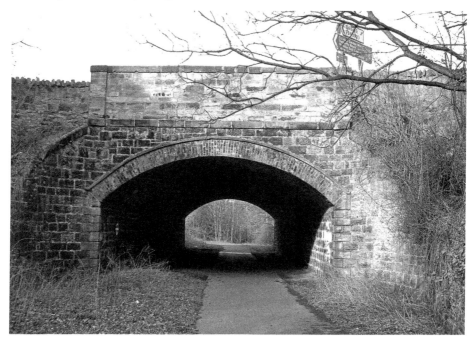

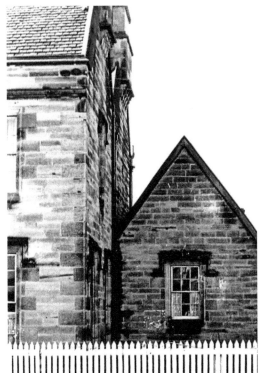

Opened in 1849 along with the Hawick Branch of the NBR, Eskbank Station replaced an earlier station on the original Marquis of Lothian's Tramway. The main station building was designed in a grand style to satisfy the Marquis. Constructed over two stories, it housed the ticket office and entrance façade from street level along with being the station master's residence. In this 1969 photograph the northern gable and adjoining wing are seen.

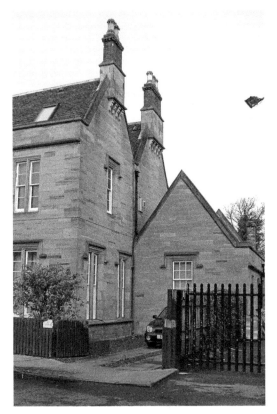

Few exterior modifications have been made to the structure since the line was closed. The building is now in use as flats and has benefitted from a much-needed cleaning of over 100 years of soot and general pollution.

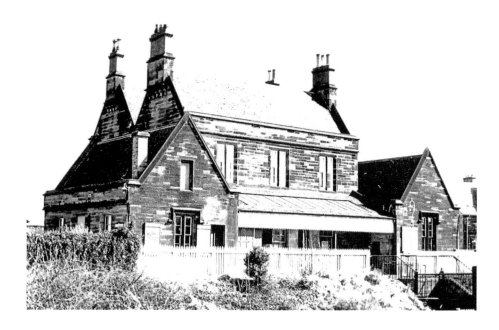

The main line side elevation can be seen in its entirety here. The canopy allowed for a modicum of shelter for passengers before either descending the steps to the up platform or crossing the footbridge for the Edinburgh-bound down platform.

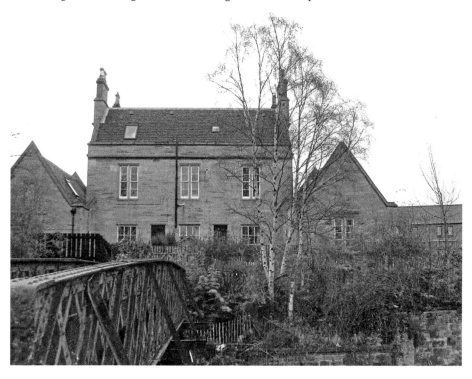

This 2005 study has had to be taken from a more direct elevation due to tree growth over the intervening years. The only noticeable differences are the removal of the canopy and the almost iridescent nature of the now cleaned stonework.

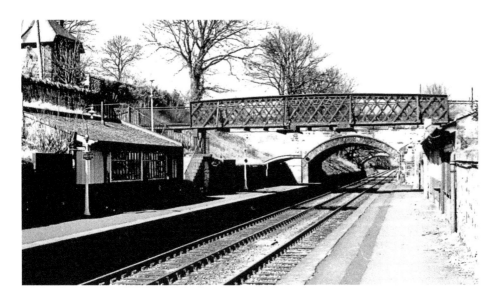

A view north from the up platform. Here we see the trackside layout of the station with, left to right, the Edinburgh down platform with attendant recessed waiting room and smaller curved roof shelter beyond for the morning commuters; metal footbridge, which was removed in July of 2012; and the up platform and recessed waiting room. The main station building is to the right at street level. Lasswade Road, Bridge 14, stands steadfast behind.

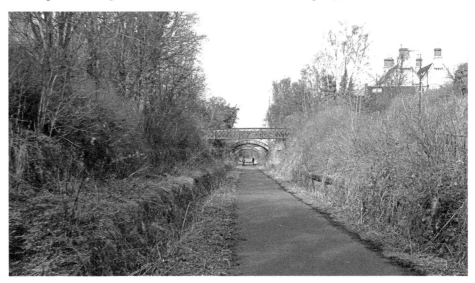

Despite the construction of the footpath, the overgrown nature of the platforms is quite apparent here. The new Borders Railway will at least see Eskbank put back onto the railway map although a more suitable site has been identified, behind the camera, on which to site the new station.

A group, of which the authors are members, was kindly donated the footbridge structure for reuse at Whitrope, to the south of Hawick. The WRHA/BURC is indebted to Transport Scotland, The Projects and to the members of the WRHA who oversaw its safe removal and transportation to our site. It is hoped to restore the structure and reuse it again in the not too distant future.

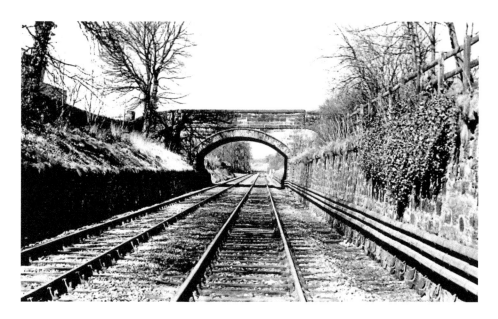

Gilmerton Road overbridge is located just to the north of Eskbank Station, in the same cutting. From here it was a short run to Glenesk Junction, where the original Innocent Railway diverged to Dalkeith. At this point the River North Esk is crossed, which earned the town its name. A beautiful wooded valley is crossed high above by the route at this point, in stark contrast to the cutting the station platforms lie within.

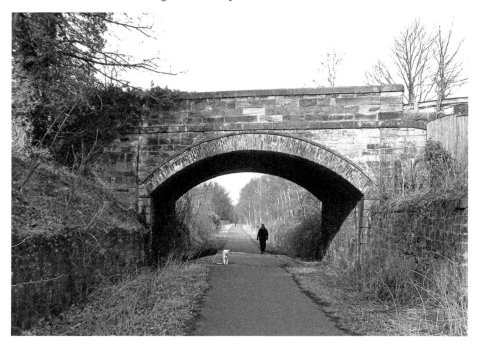

Seen here again in 2005, it is just possible to make out the parapet of Glenesk Viaduct through Gilerton Road bridge. Glenesk Junction was located to the right hand side, almost immediately towards the camera, and was flanked to the left by a set of sidings for local collieries and merchants.

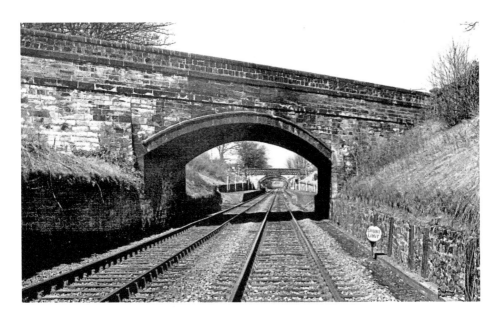

A trackside northern view through Bonnyrigg Road from Hardengreen Junction, affording an observation as to just how close a relationship these locations had to each other. To the right is the 'limit of shunt' board for the up sidings at Hardengreen; we can then see the Eskbank Station platforms and footbridge, followed by Lasswade Road and Gilmerton Road bridges, culminating with Glenesk Junction and viaduct at the track horizon.

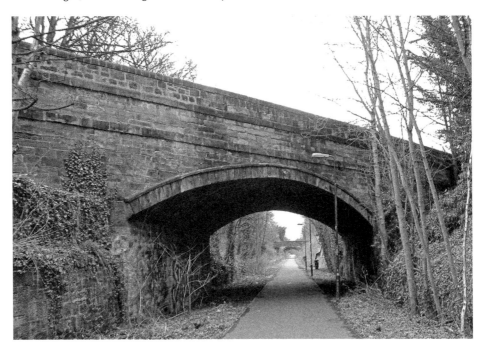

In the intervening years, despite the loss of track and ballast, the locations are instantly recognisable. The new Eskbank Station will be sited a little behind the camera. Given the presence of planned double track through this location, it is currently unclear if any of the masonry overbridges are to be retained.

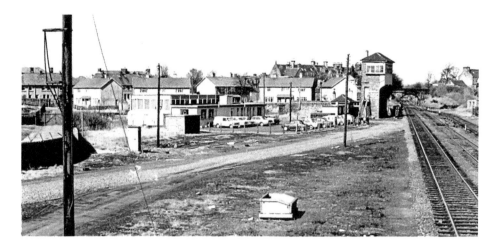

Hardengreen Junction was the location from which the Peebles loop diverged from the Waverley Route. This loop returned back to the line at Kilnknowe Junction in Galashiels. The Penicuik and Poulton branches both diverged within a matter of miles from the Peebles loop, and with the presence early on of a branch to Smeaton the location was the centre of quite some activity, warranting a sub shed out base of St Margarets, the main route traction provider. This sub shed provided locomotives for local freight duties and for banking assistance for heavy freight traffic to Falahill, with the gradient stiffening here after.

The loop can be seen as a clear grey mark to the left, having already been lifted by this stage, and the former Smeaton branch is indicated by the tightly curving wall to the right of the existing tracks. By this date, again 1969, severe rationalisation of the area had already been undertaken but the over-sailing lofty signal box is an indicator of the former junction's importance.

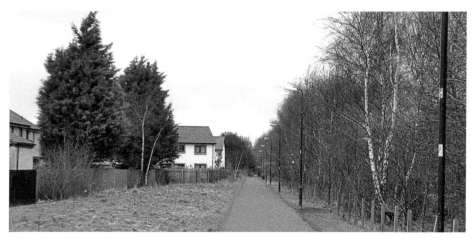

Unfortunately, the current lack of signals prevents such an exact replication today. It is, however, possible to still identify the location with Bonnyrigg Road bridge and the footpath from Sherifhall running through the site.

Today, a housing estate occupies the former Peebles Loop and all traces bar a few have been landscaped away from the 1969 study. The good news, however, is that this is to be the location of the new Eskbank Station and attendant car park. With the dramatic expansion of residential properties in this area, I would hope the addition of rail, as an alternative to travel by car or bus, is at least felt most welcome here.

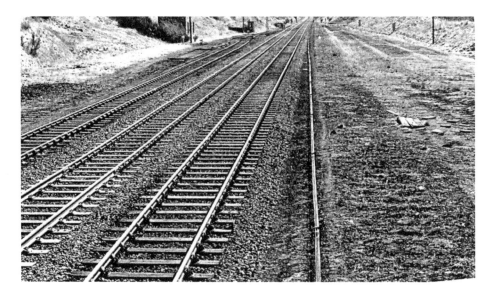

This is the corresponding view south for the previous 1969 shot. The expanse of siding space now becomes quite apparent. Four running loops had existed to the right or Edinburgh-bound side here, for the provision of marshalling freight from local merchants and coal from the myriad of local collieries. This formed the staple work for the sub shed, along with the aforementioned banking. Two lines had existed to the left hand side for a small yard and to service the locomotives. The water tank base is still evident here despite having spent some 5 years out of use.

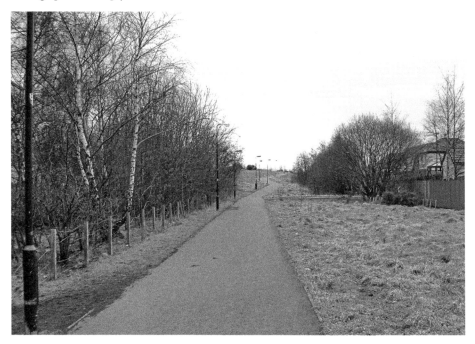

The footpath and housing continues but little else remains to the south at this location now. The footpath terminates at Harden Green Farm overbridge, which still exists, minus its north elevation parapet, within the in-filled and landscaped cutting seen ahead.

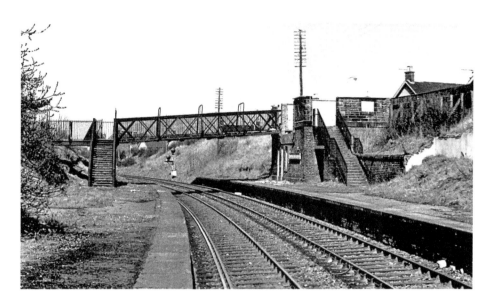

Newtongrange Station was a relatively late arrival on the route, being constructed in 1908 to serve the expanding coal fields. Prior to this date little more than a hamlet had existed in this area, with only a few small pits. The subsequent vast expansion of the Lady Victoria Pit saw a huge increase in housing in what is now a suburb of Edinburgh in its own right.

The station's main building, demolished by the time of this view, had stood at street level and partially over sailed the up platform. The last remnants of the route were removed from the railway map through here some three years after the line's official demise: the stub remaining to the two last productive collieries in this area.

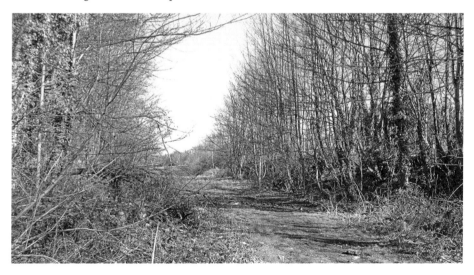

As recently as the mid to late 1990s it had been possible to walk through the platforms here on what had become a very wet formation. Local landscaping works to improve the link between two housing schemes and the village centre saw the removal of the footbridge and the partial infilling of the platform area.

Newtongrange, however, is another location which will benefit from the railway's rejuvenation, receiving, as it will, a new station as little as 30 yards to the south of the original site.

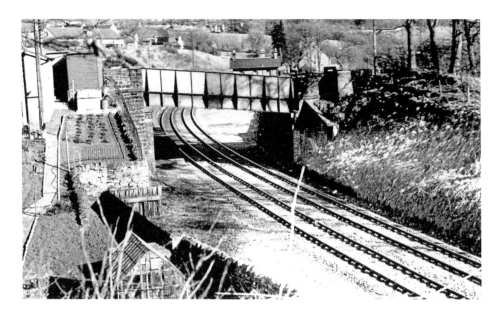

The northen approach to Gorebridge Station in 1969. The severe curvature of the route is evident in this photograph. Gorebridge Station was built on a 27-chain curve but was at least graced with being on a short level section of line. The up platform is evident, commencing beneath Station Road bridge, and the main station building can be seen above.

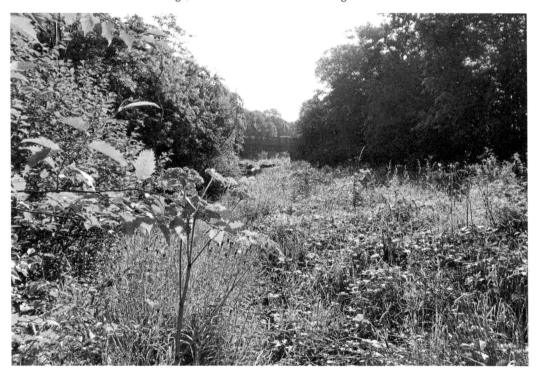

A true comparison is not possible today due to the amount of tree growth. The cutting has lightly back filled and the area is overgrown and very wet – a challenge that the contractors for the new Borders Railway will have to overcome.

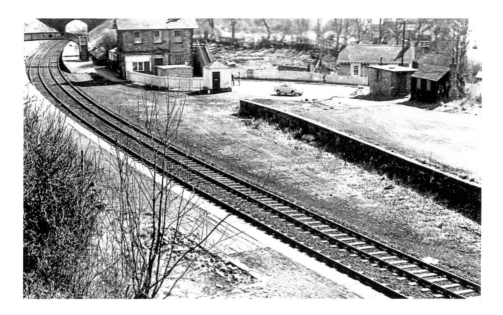

The staggered nature of the platforms can be seen here, along with the old goods yard. The goods yard had originally contained three sidings, one being an engine release for shunting. Unlike other goods facilities, this yard could be accessed from both up and down lines. The scar from the demolished signal box can be seen on the up platform, at the left centre foreground. This box closed along with the yard in March 1965.

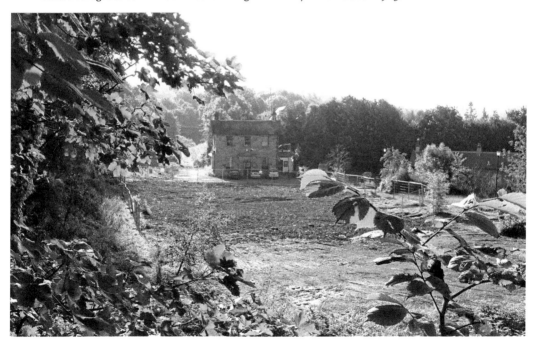

It is not possible to see from this 2012 shot, but both platforms are still extent although back filled. Until the early summer of 2012 a housing complex known as Haviston Villas had stood on the site of the goods yard and main line formation. These have now been demolished to make way for the new railway.

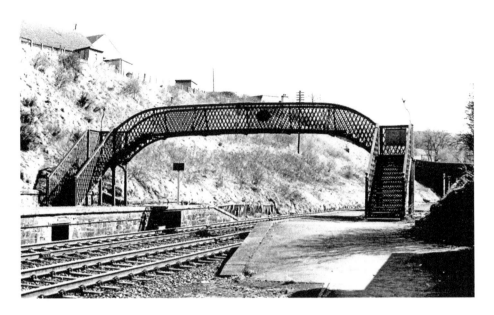

Gorebridge Station footbridge is seen straddling the very short section of overlap between the two platforms. The down platform seen on the right is to be rebuilt on a slightly altered alignment and is to become the new Gorebridge Station.

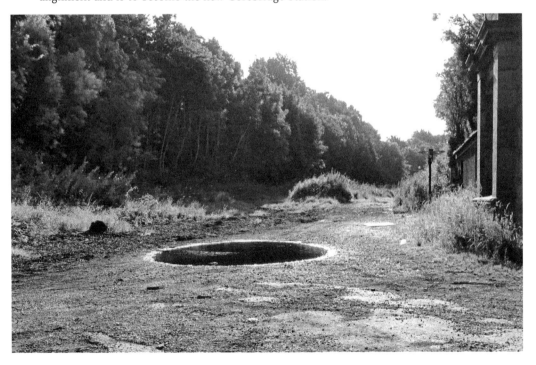

The contemporary photograph shows well the infilling undertaken in this area. The footbridge lingered on well into the 1970s before being removed. No such structure will be required with the new build at at this location – it is to be single track.

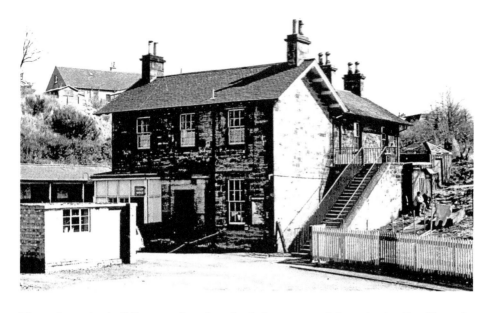

The main station building, seen here in 1969. A short approach from Station Road brought passengers to this fine two-storey building. The platforms were accessed via the booking office until the station was downgraded to an unstaffed halt in 1967.

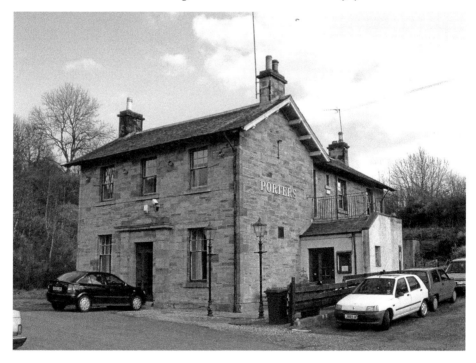

The main building was retained with minimal alterations and is seen here in 2005 in use as a restaurant, aptly named Porters.

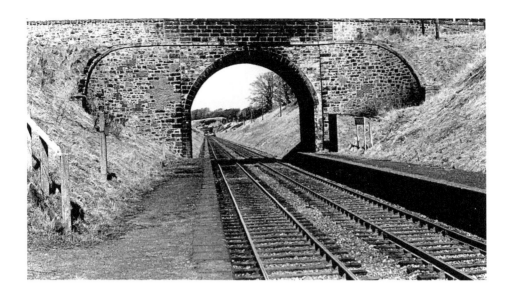

A broadly rural area indeed. Only with the coming of the railway did a small hamlet grow up in its vicinity. As with further south of Hawick, the NBR tried as best they could in the more sparsely populated areas to provide centralised goods facilities for the local agricultural markets. Station facilities were always provided but I would suspect the Directors realised that very little passenger traffic would materialise. With this in mind, it comes as quite a surprise that despite the loss of goods facilities in November 1963 Tynehead was retained to the end, albeit with vastly reduced service and as an unstaffed halt.

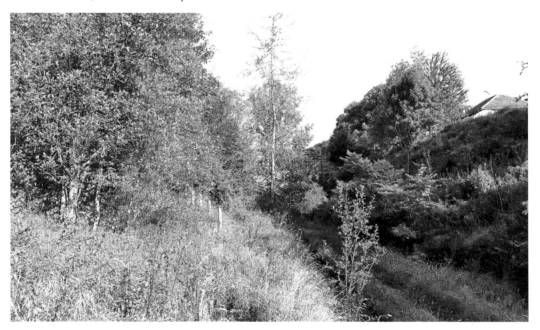

As can be seen from both photographs, the location remains largely unchanged. In the vast undergrowth both platforms survive and the down platform access is still discernable by its concrete fence posts. The station is situated in a deep cutting a mile in length with a three-quarter-mile straight, a rarity on the whole route, although on the fearsome 1:70 gradient.

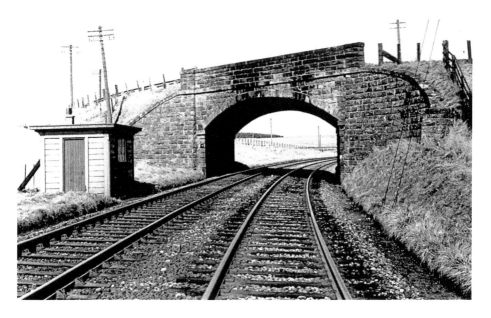

Bridge 44 took the A7 road over the route, just to the south of Falahill Summit. This location was included due to the relative camera-shy nature of the structure. The road was forced into a double dog leg to cross the line on a skew masonry bridge, as shown in this 1969 BURC study.

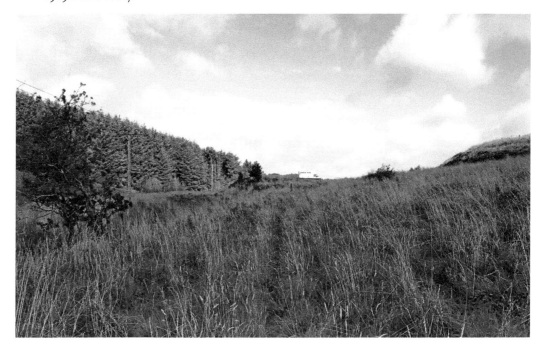

The location proved to be a bottle neck, slowing traffic down, on closure of the route. As much as the structure is missed, it has to be said that the decision to remove it and realign the road at this location was a sensible one. Unfortunately for the Border community, the rest of the promised road improvements post-closure are still yet to materialise. A double track line will once again see the road realigned here.

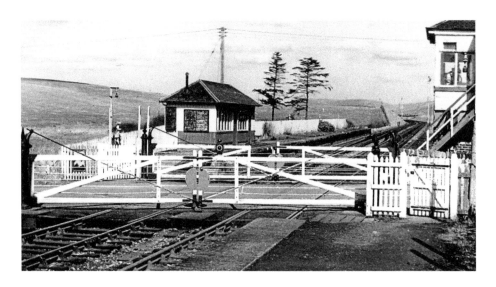

Another broadly rural area, at the head of the Gala Valley, Heriot at least served a small rural community with its platforms staggered either side of its level crossing. The down platform was to the north, with the main station building, signal box and a very small yard consisting of two sidings opposite. The up platform on the south side of the level crossing spanned the Gala Water along with the line at its mid-point. Just over a mile south of Falahill Summit, it represented a relaxing run down to Galashiels for firemen of south-bound trains and nearly the end of the climb for Edinburgh-bound traffic, albeit at much more forgiving gradients.

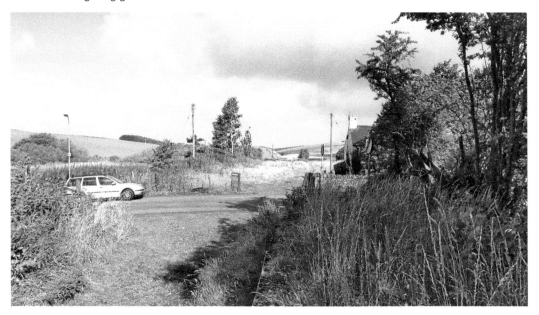

Today only the up platform remains, with the down platform north of the level crossing having been landscaped some time ago by the previous owner of the station house. An underpass is to be built here and the level crossing will be consigned to history due to the proximity of the main A7 trunk route. It is understood at the time of writing that a new road will be built to serve the village further to the south. No new station is to be built here.

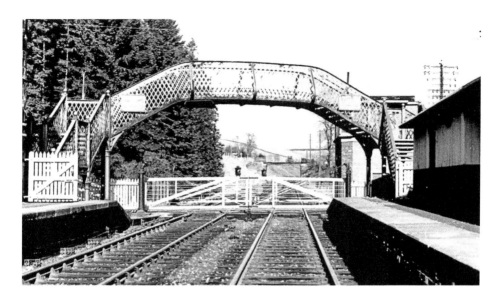

Fountainhall was another location with a level crossing, as illustrated here. Looking north, the station was located with its attendant footbridge on the south side of the level crossing, with the box on the north side. Fountainhall became a junction with the opening of the Lauder branch in 1901 although this closed to passengers in the 1930s. The branch lingered on for freight into the late 1950s.

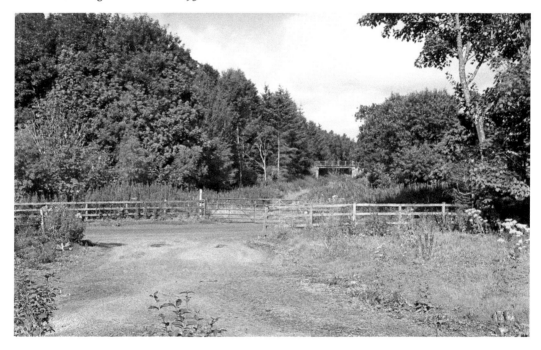

With the closure of the route to passengers in January 1969, Fountainhall Station fell out of use. Freight traffic lingered on as far as Hawick until the April of the same year; however, with the closure of all signal boxes south of Lady Victoria Pit the trainman and guard became responsible for the opening of all level crossing gates. The line, for this short 4-month period, was effectively being worked as a long siding.

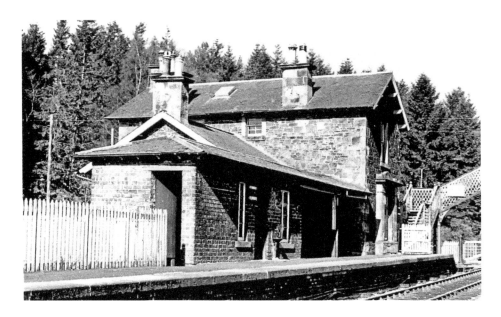

The main station building was quite a substantial structure. Constructed over three storeys, ground out of site below, first at platform level and the second above, it was quite an imposing structure for what was in essence a rural backwater. The line was finally lifted here in 1971 and the station abandoned to its fate.

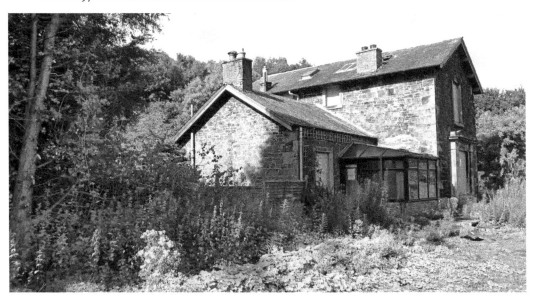

After a period out of use, the station was converted into a private residence and sensitively converted into a domestic dwelling. As can be seen from this contemporary study, with the exception of the waiting shelter very little has changed. The down platform is still extant, although in-filled, in the vicinity of the main building but the up platform, footbridge and waiting room have been demolished to form a landscaped garden area. The property is now vacant while the new construction works take place. Transport Scotland are hoping that on completion of these works a new owner can be found.

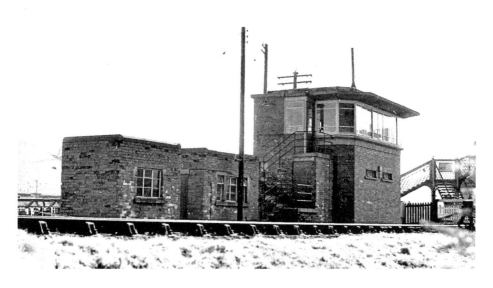

The signal box was relocated to the up side and to the north of the level crossing in 1954. This BR-built box is shown to good effect here and puts one in mind of the old Hornby/Meccano box, which was also produced in the 1950s.

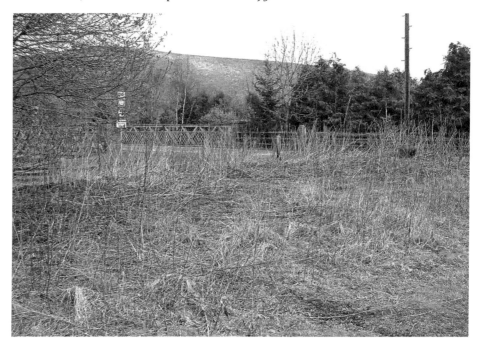

The signal box, being only 15 years old and therefore relatively modern, was stripped of all mechanical and electrical instruments for reuse elsewhere shortly after closure. Demolition then followed in the early 1970s. As can be seen, only the bridge girder to the left ties the two photographs together.

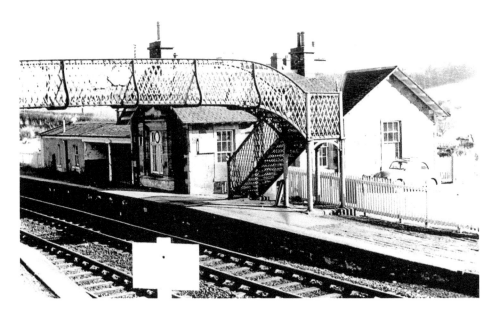

Stow was another station built on a tight curve, 36 chains in this instance, and in a cutting. The loco crews were at least afforded some respite here as it was on a quarter-mile level section, allowing a run at the bank to be made for north-bound services. Opening with the Hawick branch in 1849, the station lasted through until final closure in 1969.

A fine three-quarters study of the main building is shown here, illustrating well the single-storey masonry construction.

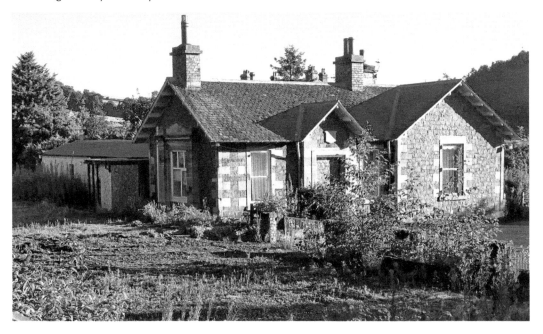

Although currently empty, the main building survives with marginal alterations in 2012. The waiting shelter has been converted into an annex and a porch provided onto the in filled platforms. Only the footbridge, clock and, obviously, the track are really missing from the contemporary scene. The track, however, is set to return in 2014.

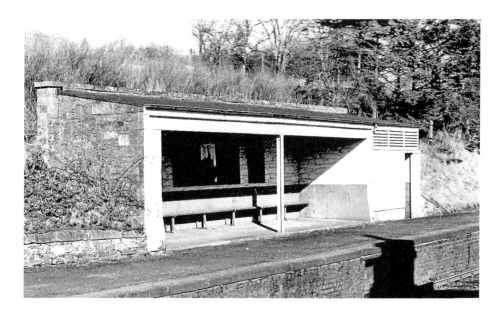

The down waiting room at Stow was another recessed affair. Again, the use of white-washing can be seen in an attempt to lighten the dark recesses.

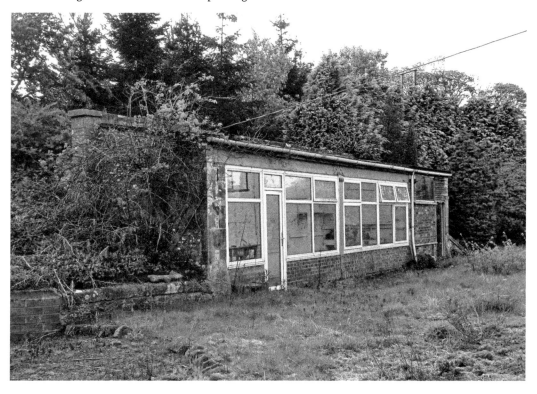

This author has witnessed many ingenious uses for old structures but converting a waiting shelter into a greenhouse has to rank pretty high up on the unusual scale. The conversion has at least succeeded where the NBR and BR failed, making the interior very light and most welcoming.

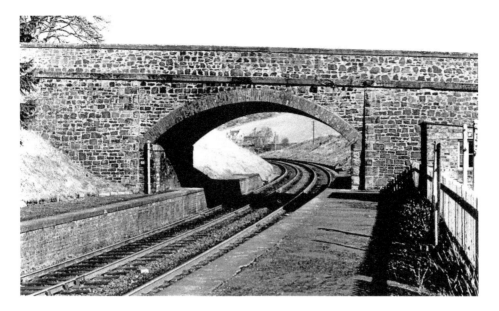

The curvature is shown to good effect here as we look north under Station Road bridge. The platforms were very slightly staggered and, as can be seen, continued beyond Bridge 68.

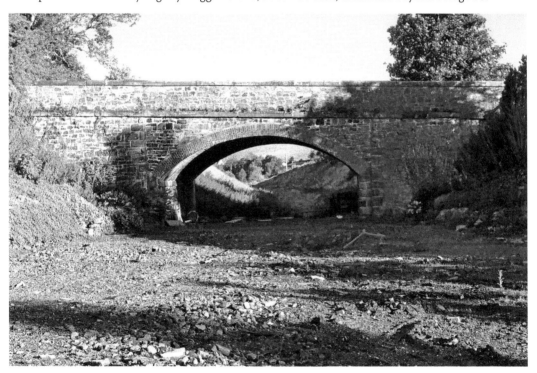

Until early 2012 a house had stood directly in the way of this contemporary view. Quite what inspired the decision to grant planning approval for the construction of a domestic dwelling slap bang in the middle of a former railway is anyone's guess. Thankfully for the reinstatement and unfortunately for the house's owner, this situation has now been resolved, as can be seen by the scar on the ground.

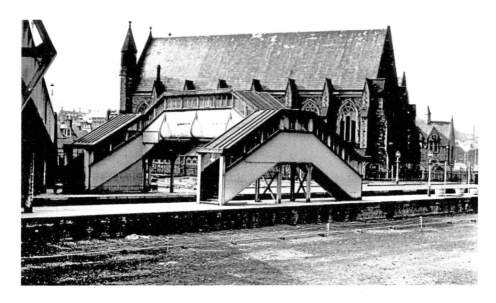

Only Hawick and St Boswells have suffered the same degree of destruction of former railway infrastructure as Galashiels, although absolutely no trace remains at Galashiels of the station. The key linking building for this series of photographs is the church.

The north end of the platforms contained the footbridge as seen here and the Station Brae road bridge bisected the site at a skewed angle.

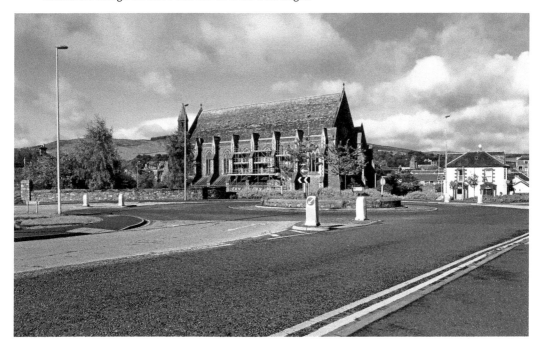

The station site was quickly cleared and over time has given way to road improvements, as can be seen here. These have taken place over a number of years and in the mid-2000s Station Brae was removed as it was deemed life expired.

Scottish Borders Council provided a new replacement structure in anticipation of the new Borders Railway.

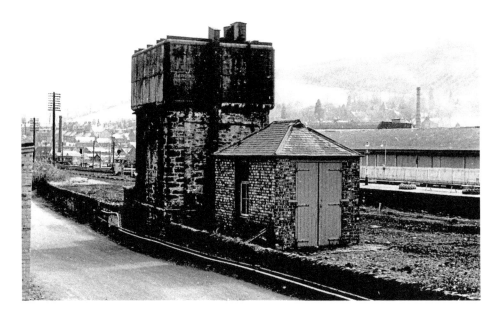

The station's water tower stood to the north side of the station complex. Galashiels was located 33½ miles from Edinburgh and at the foot of a 15½-mile climb to Falahill Summit for north-bound services. This was the last opportunity to take on water for the climb.

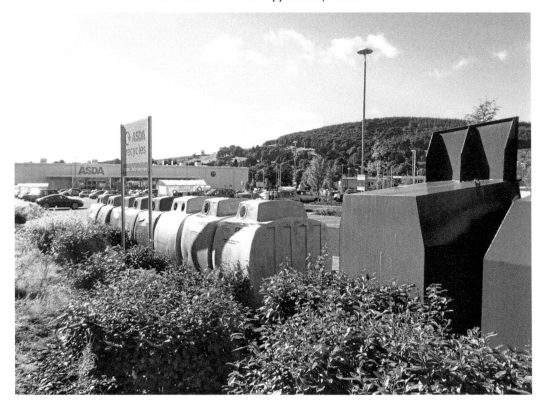

Today the whole site has been erased, giving way to the almost standard supermarket complex so loved of modern society. The water tower's location is now a recycling centre.

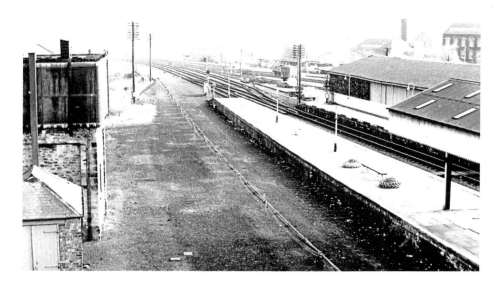

The view south shows to good advantage the large goods yard and the island platform. Galashiels had three platforms as it was the junction for the returning Peebles loop and the branch to Selkirk.

The Peebles loop was closed to all traffic in 1962 and the Selkirk branch closed to passengers in 1951 and to freight in 1964. The branch traffic originally departed from Platform 3, seen in the foreground here with the track lifted.

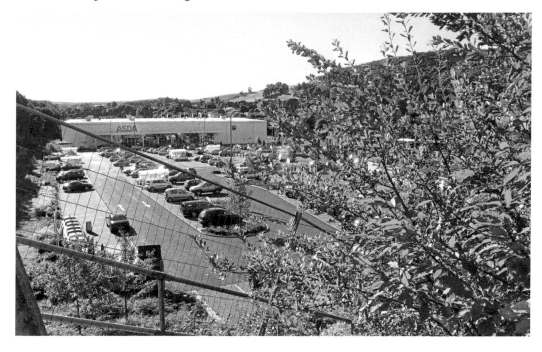

The main line originally ran through the right hand side of the superstore and curved round alongside the Gala Water. The new build will run along the left of this view, passing the store on a new alignment. It does not look feasible from this view but enough room exists for a single track and the line speed will be relatively low at this point.

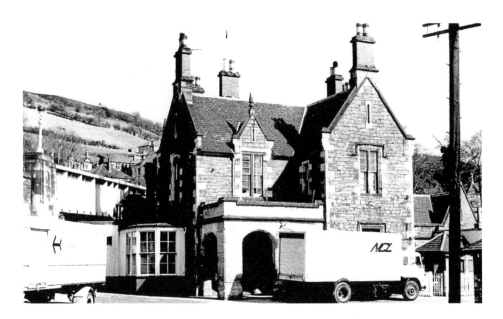

The main station building is shown to good effect here. It is possible to see the juxtaposition of Station Brae to the main station infrastructure. The importance of this location is well demonstrated by the sizable goods yard shown on pages 40 and 41. Gala was consequently one of the main hubs of traffic for the route, being situated on a series of junctions, as previously mentioned.

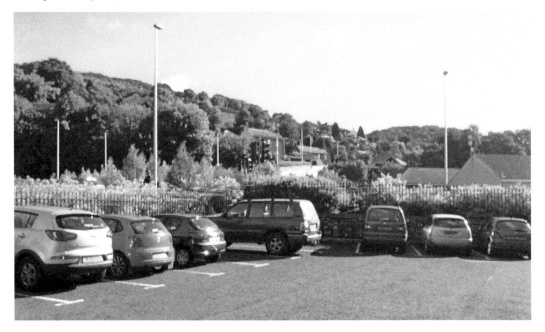

September 2012 and the winner of the 'spot the car' competition is this author. Decimation would be the only true or fair analogy for the wholesale destruction that has occurred between the historic and contemporary views. Apparently this is to be called progress?

2014 will hopefully bring the reverberation of rail traction back to this scene, although hidden behind the trees.

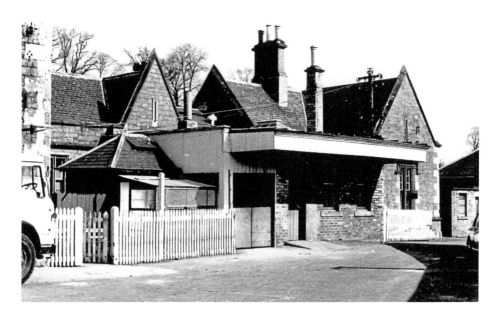

A further study of the main station buildings at Gala. By this date, April 1969, the line was still open to freight traffic (just) and National Carriers Limited still plied their trade from this hub.

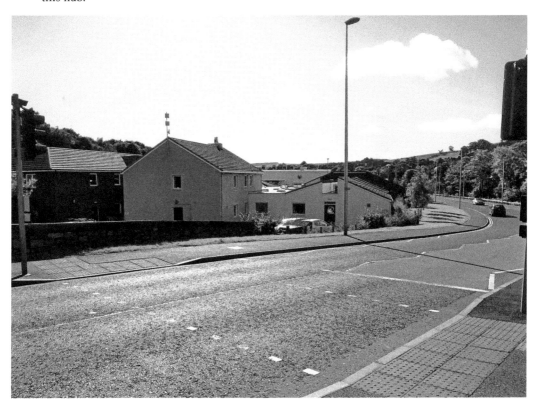

Unfortunately, a very different definition of 'crossing the road' is to be found at this location today. I would surmise this is called progress, of a fashion.

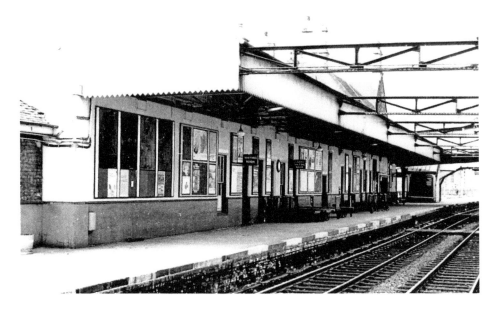

Platform 1. With what could only be considered as unreasonable haste, this façade was unduly consigned to history shortly after closure.

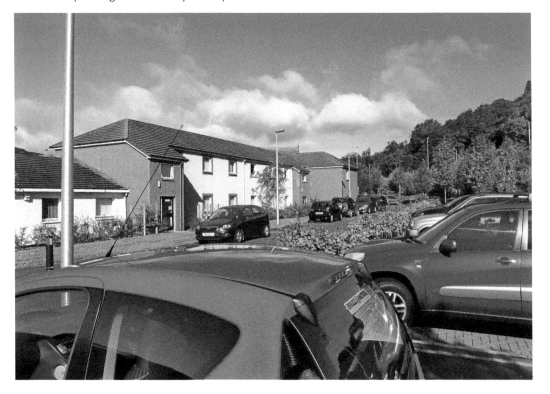

Today, a health centre exists on this site. Not in itself a bad replacement, but the architecture is somewhat lacking compared to its predecessor in this author's opinion.

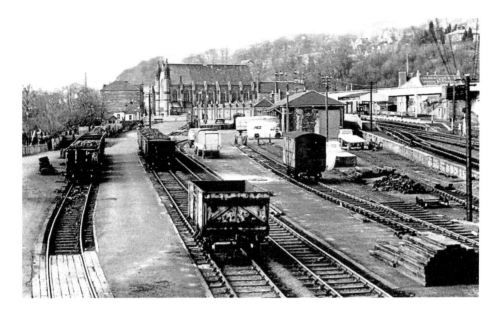

Despite the run-down feel of the goods yard here, it is clear to see the nature of traffic both generated and delivered to Galashiels. Coal contained in 16-ton mineral wagons is predominant to the left and through the centre. A 12-ton general merchandise van occupies another road.

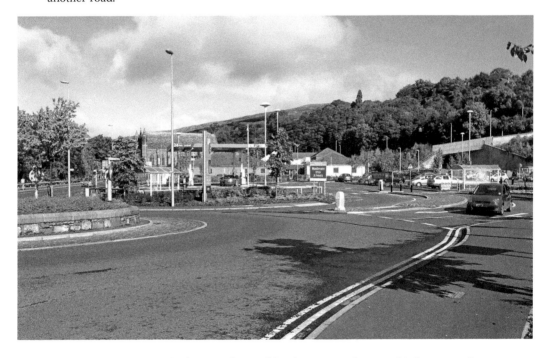

Absolute decimation of the historical record has been carried out at this location. The one positive from a railwayman's point of view is the provision of a replacement structure for Station Brae, as can be seen in the right background. I personally would struggle to described the changes witnessed here. Unless the reader is mad on roundabouts, there is very little I could say.

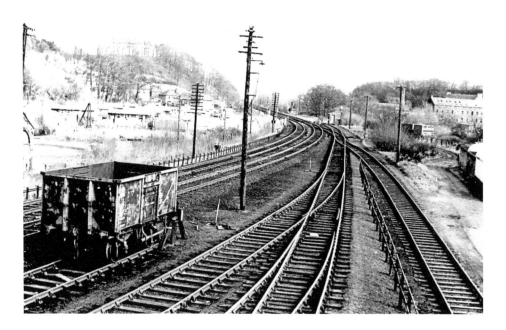

The view south, or strictly speaking west, from the goods yard throat. Three quarters of a mile to the south was Selkirk Junction, which was retained for freight. The town of Selkirk was, like Galashiels, a major source of textiles which contributed to rail-born freight from the central Borders.

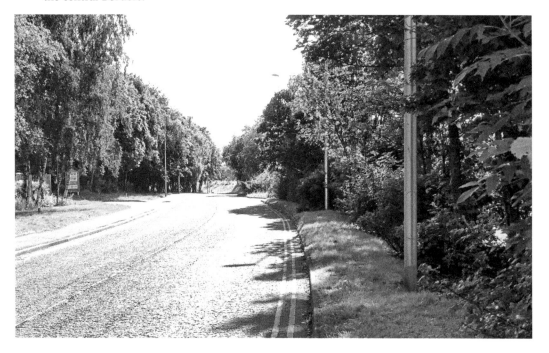

A very pleasant avenue of trees now stands proud, flanking, as it does, the road. The former route is defined by the grass embankment at the road's divergence. Unfortunately, an elevated comparison is not currently possible without climbing trees. I personally gave that pastime up some years ago and moved on to Lego.

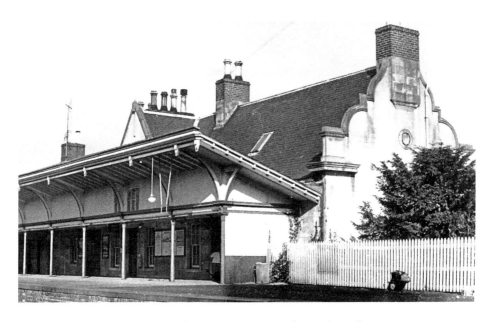

The main station building at Melrose was constructed over three floors.

The ground floor housed the entrance and a flight of steps up to the first floor platform landing and an attic space existed above. Designed with no small amount of grandeur, Melrose Station's main building befitted this Abbey town.

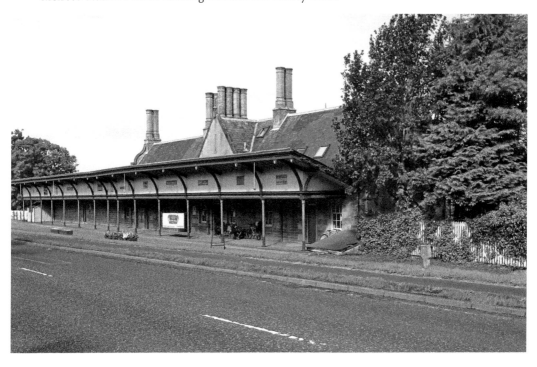

A new bypass was constructed along the formation in 1987, sweeping away the down platform. It is not, however, all bad news. The Victorian cast iron gentlemen's toilet block from the down platform is preserved on the Severn Valley Railway, although it is not currently in use, and the main station building has been afforded Grade A listing.

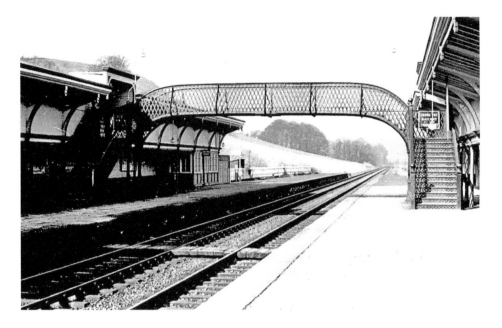

A view northbound through the picturesque but never the less deserted platforms at Melrose, one of few stations on a straight section of line and on a gentle 1:200 rising gradient towards Newtown St Boswells. Despite the ease of gradient and the racing track nature of this section of route, neither up nor down traffic had significant time to gather any speed. Melrose was one of the main stops in both directions and being 3½ miles from Gala and only a little over 2 miles from St Boswells, engine crews had little need for heroics.

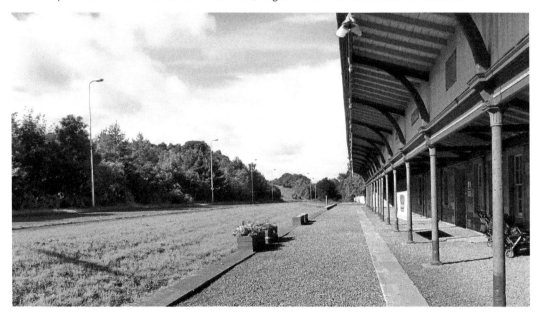

The relationship between road and former permanent way is plainly apparent here. Although the difficulties of any reinstatement are easy to observe, returning the tracks to Melrose would not be impossible. At this point in time, the return of rails south of Tweedbank is open to conjecture. No firm plans exist and the current talk is just that.

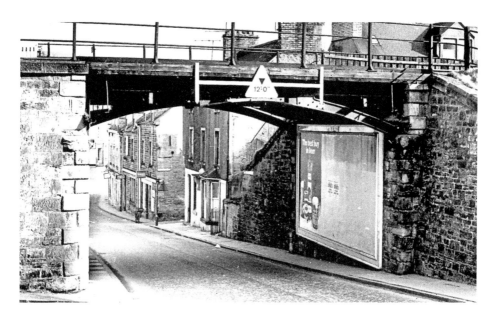

Immediately to the south of the platforms, Dingleton Road was crossed on this fine, low, cast iron bridge.

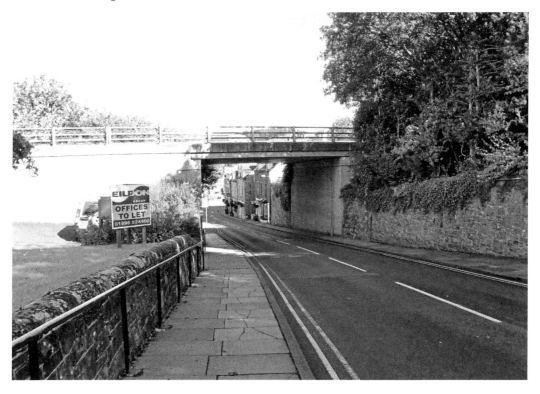

Removed with the construction of the bypass along the formation, the replacement bridge has understandably had to be raised to allow larger traffic beneath.

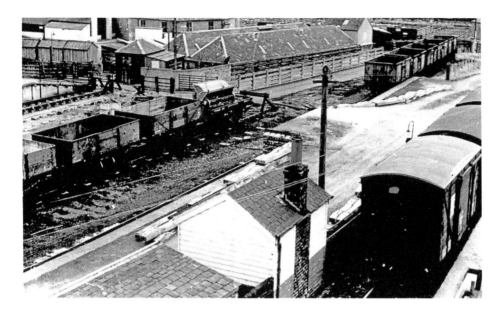

St Boswells possessed one of the largest yards on the whole route and was a source of much agricultural traffic in both cattle and machinery as well as domestic coal and fuel. This small town is the current location of the main Scottish Borders Council seat.

This first view over the yard complex illustrates well the varied nature of the goods traffic with, left to right, 12-ton open wagons and a lowfit with a cutting machine on, coal traffic slightly above and 12-ton general merchandise vans to the right foreground.

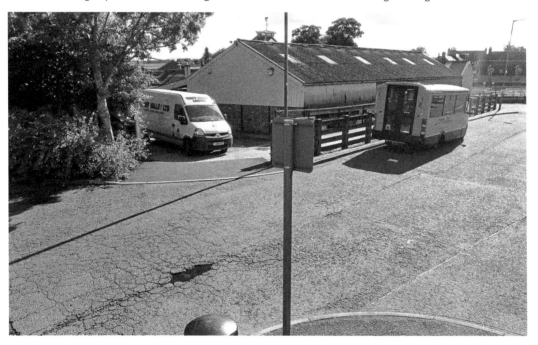

The small building above the minibus links these two scenes. St Boswells still possess a vibrant agricultural market and auction to this day. The whole area here has been redeveloped now, as we can see from the contemporary view.

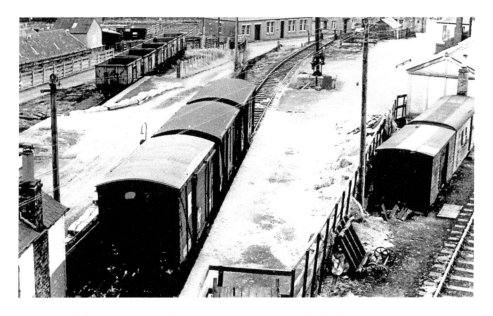

A slightly different view is afforded in this sequence. The buildings above the vans still exist to this date and tie these scenes together.

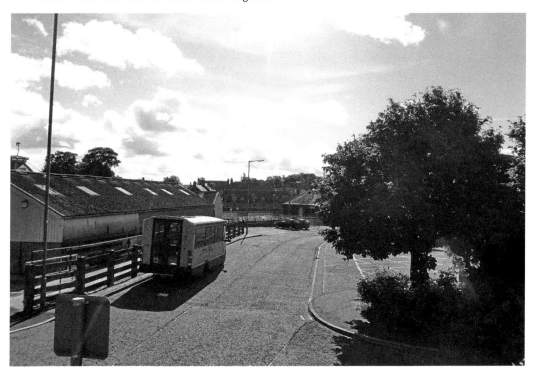

The buildings mentioned above are partially obscured by the new tree growth, the gable being visible to the left of the tree which now occupies the former goods shed site.

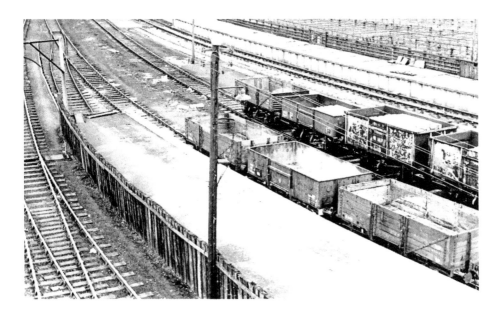

The down yard complex is seen here, looking to the north-east. The open wagons standing in the centre road appear to be loaded with concrete fence posts. The length, nature and construction of the loading docks are shown well in this study.

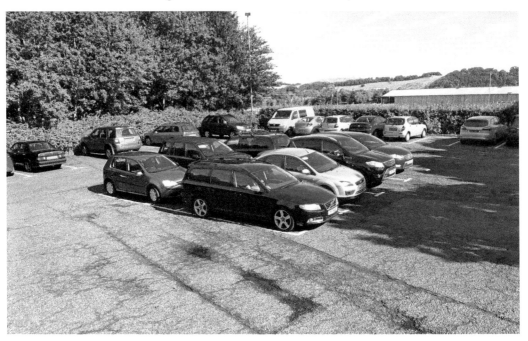

The recycle bin vantage point was again utilised for this contemporary photograph. Somewhat handy and thoughtful of the council to provide this resource at the former Up Home signal location.

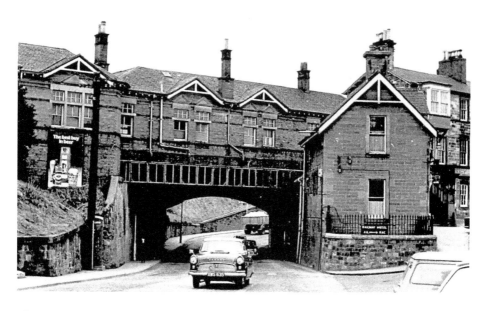

The up main station buildings and waiting rooms straddled the A68 Edinburgh Road at St Boswells, as is well illustrated in this 1969 view. Demolition commenced with undignified haste and little remains now to indicate the presence or passing of the route, a short stub of the former southern abutment being the only sign.

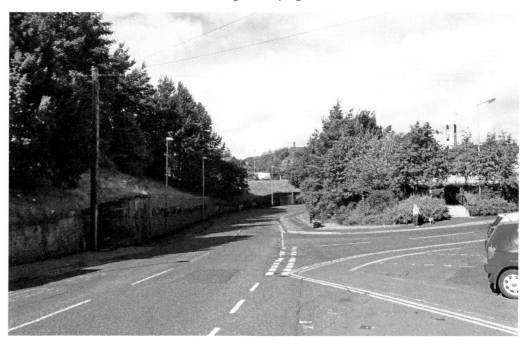

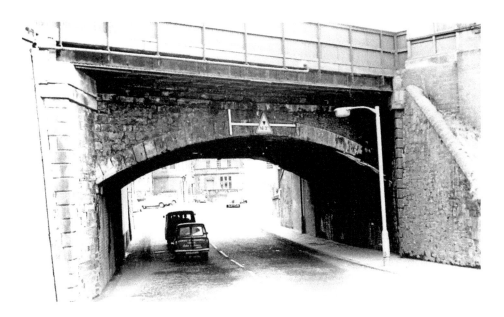

The A68 road bridge is seen again here, but from the down line side in this instance. Again, the platforms crossed this structure supported on the iron girders seen above the arch. Unlike its contemporary on the up side, no buildings crossed over the Edinburgh Road on this side.

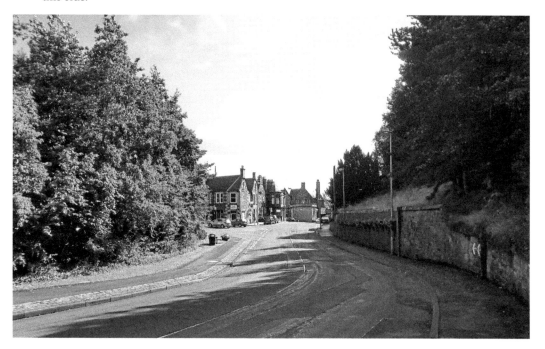

What can one say? The buildings beyond just about tie the scenes together and were it not for the abutment to the right, no comparison could be taken seriously.

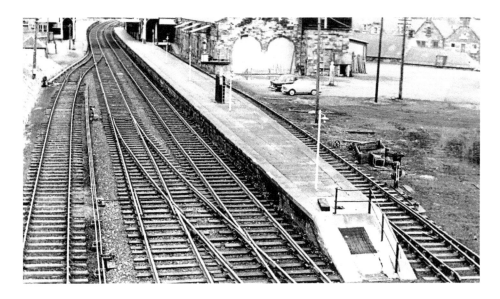

The south end of the station complex, showing the down refuge siding to the left; the main lines through the staggered platforms, centre; the bay platform for Kelso and Tweedmouth; and finally the former shed to the right hand side.

With branchs both north, from Ravenswood Junction to Greenlaw, Duns and Reston, and to the south from Kelso Junction, St Boswells was a busy location. The engine shed provided traction for all these lines including the Jedburgh branch, which diverged from the Kelso branch at Roxburgh Junction.

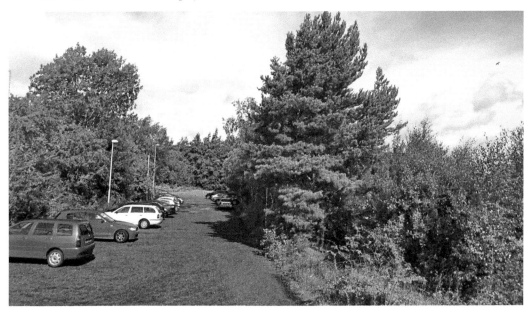

The remnants of the up main platform and bay hide within the thicket of trees to the right. The engine shed still stands, in use by the Cooks' van hire firm, hidden behind the trees along with the water tower, still sporting its cast iron top.

The contemporary view was again a test of agility, with the author being stood on the top of a fence and kissing gate to achieve some amount of elevation.

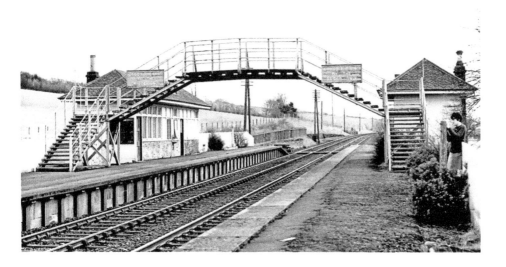

Belses was a small rural station built to serve the communities of Ancrum and Lilliesleaf, both some considerable distance away. Despite this, a well-appointed station was provided, as can be seen here.

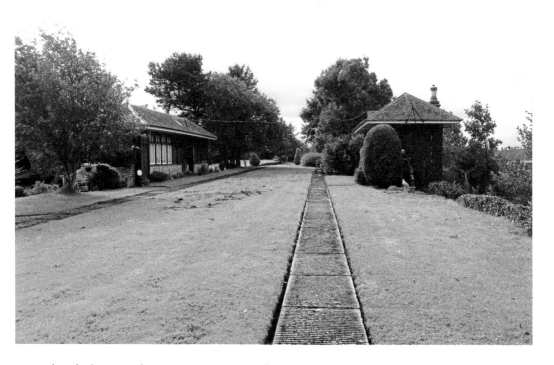

The platforms and waiting rooms are still extant and, although in-filled, a beautifully manicured garden has been created, along with a most sensitive conservation of all surviving structures, as shown through the following selection of photographs.

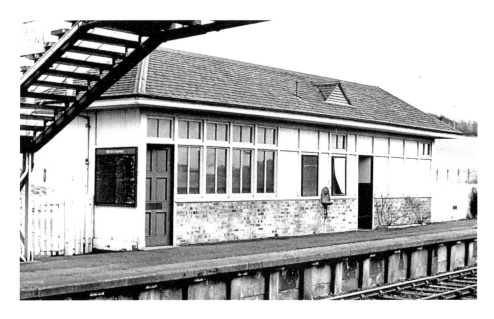

The platform elevation of the larger up waiting room. Note the NBR cast water fountain at the mid-point of the historic study.

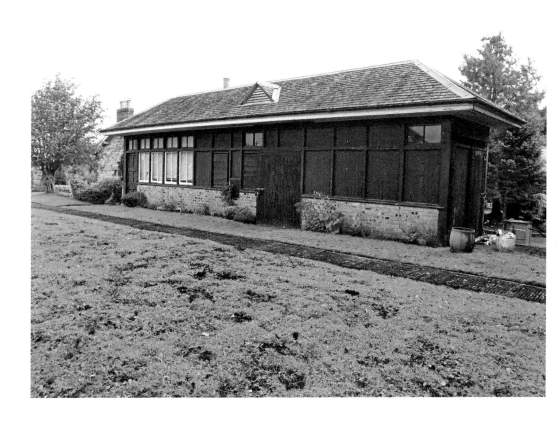

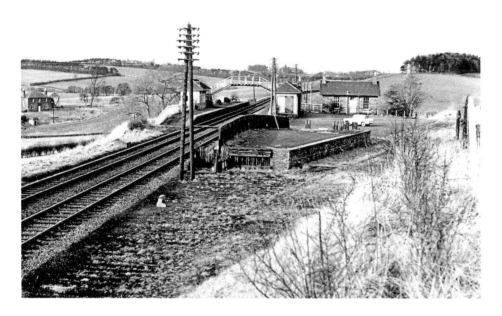

A view through the site, looking north over the former yard area with loading dock. The sparse rural nature of the area is plainly evident. The loading dock still exists, lying within the garden area.

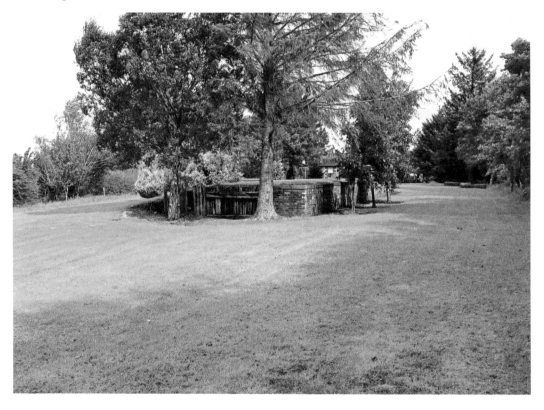

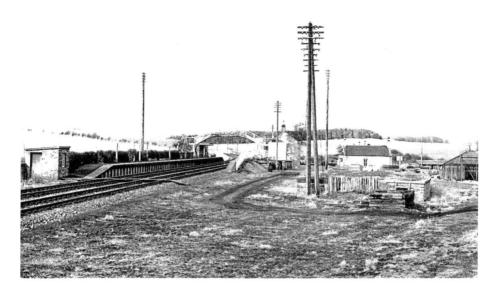

A general view looking north through the station site from the old yard area. The staggered nature of the platforms is evident and the two-storey nature of the main station building can be seen.

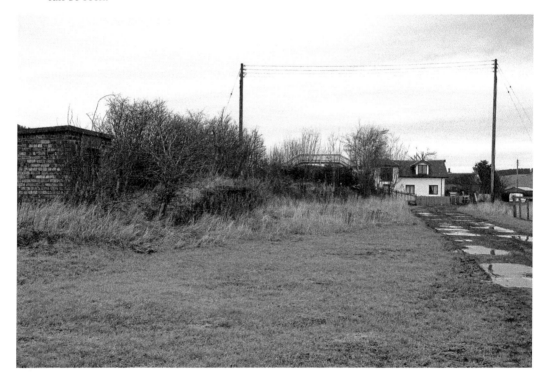

Bought by a local architect in the mid-1990s, the station house and attendant waiting shelters have all been restored and he is currently raising funds to restore the footbridge. Along with Stobs, this is the only location to retain such a feature, although the construction here is of wood and bullhead rail, quite unlike the purely rail construction of Stobs footbridge.

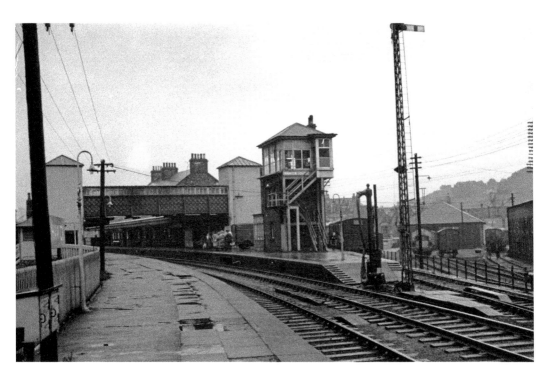

A 1969 photograph showing the Hawick South Signal Box and some of the station buildings. Some writers allege that the goods shed, to the right of the signal post, middle distance, was the original terminal station from 1849; however this writer remains unconvinced.

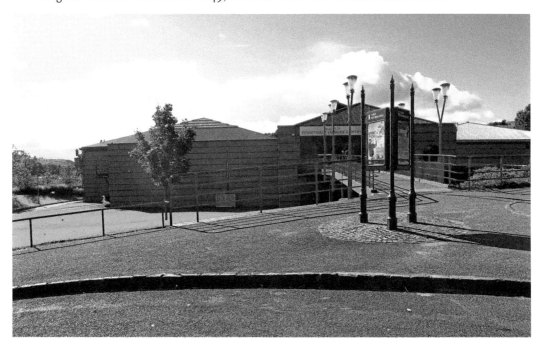

A similar view in 2012 and all trace of the railway and its station have vanished, to be replaced by Teviotdale Leisure Centre. The railway station was on the left of this photograph.

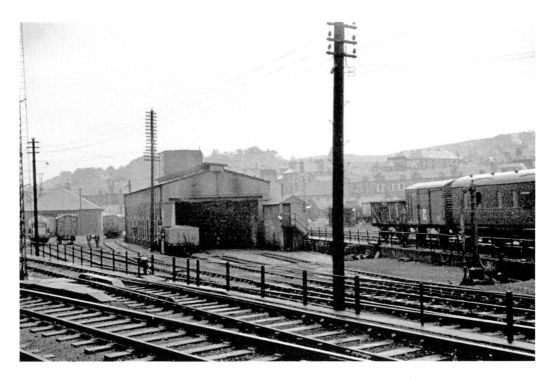

The engine shed at Hawick in 1963; closure is still over six years away but the increasing dieselisation of the train services has meant that there is no sign of the smoke and bustle which used to be its trademark.

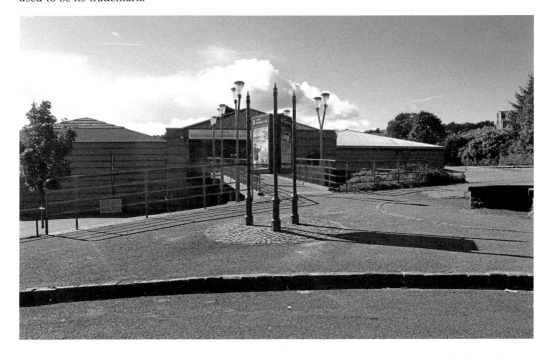

No locomotives or engine shed, nor any trace of either remains in 2012; the engine shed would have stood to the right of centre in this view.

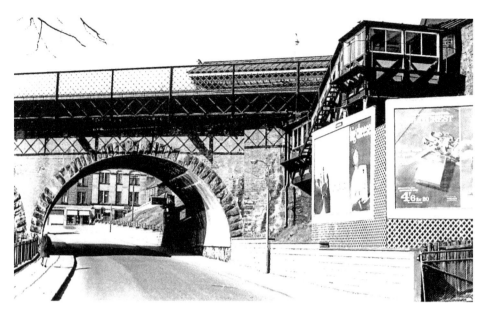

The view along Mansfield Road, Hawick, showing how the northernmost arch of Teviot Viaduct spanned the road before crossing the River Teviot. Atop the viaduct can seen the awning on the station's down platform, while closer to the camera is the little-known subway which linked the platforms.

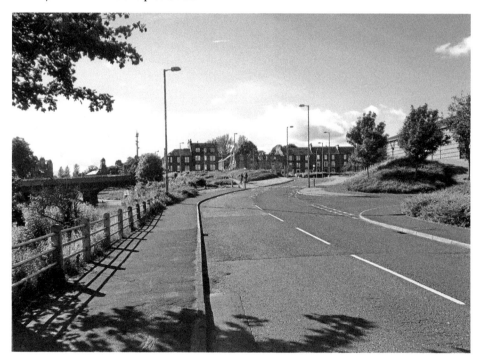

2012, and even the Teviot Viaduct has been swept away, leaving a much clearer vista to the south. Hardly a trace of the viaduct or station remains.

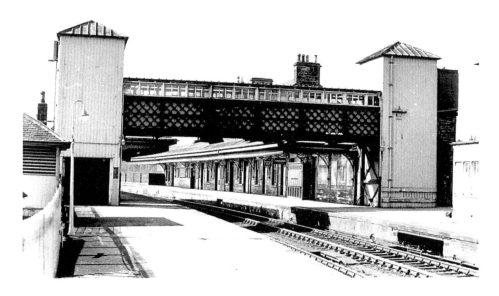

Looking south along the up platform in Hawick in 1969, this photo from opposite Hawick South Signal Box shows the station buildings and, in the foreground, the 'luggage lift' which linked the two platforms.

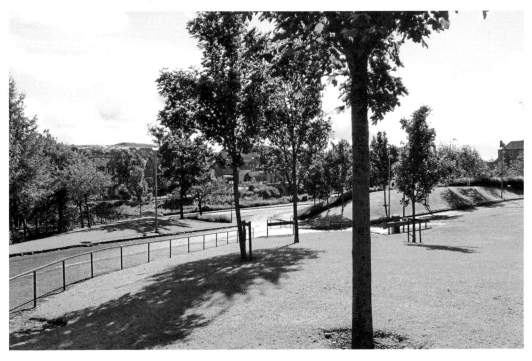

The nicely landscaped area outside the leisure centre which has replaced the station.

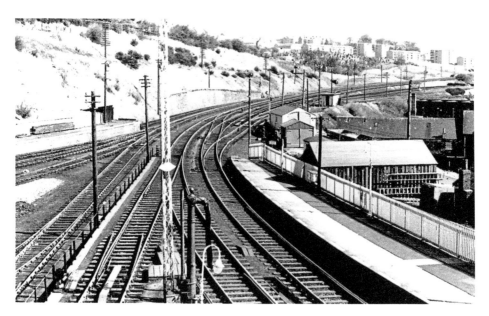

The northern approaches to Hawick showing the entrance to the gas works on the extreme right; the carriage cleaning sidings; and, nearer to the camera, from left the parcels bay, the entrance to the goods yard and the loading bank.

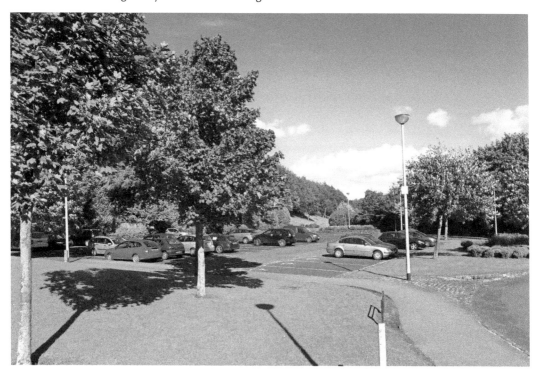

By 2012 a neatly laid out car park now adorns the area.

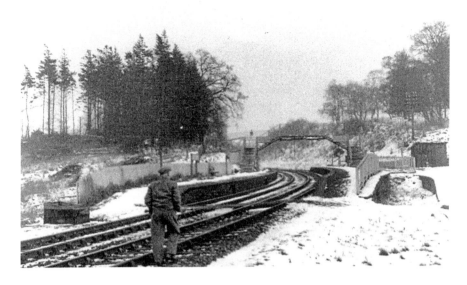

Stobs Station platforms, looking south here in 1965 with Wullie Henderson inspecting the scene. The line climbs its way through the Slitrig Valley on its way to Whitrope Summit.

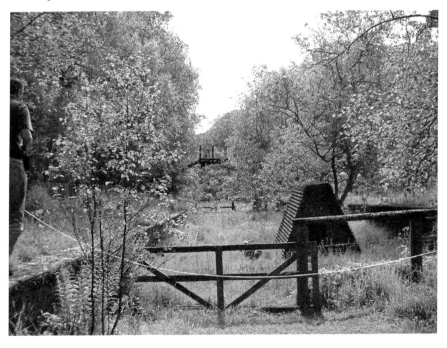

Now substantially overgrown, both platforms remain along with the footbridge seen through the trees in the background. The 1966 passenger figures here were noted to be just two passengers per week.

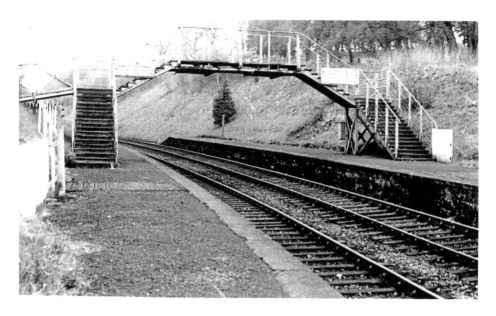

The footbridge is studied here. Constructed from bullhead rail and cast metal parts, this sturdy structure survives to the present day; however the wood used for the decking has rotted and is unsafe as such. Again safe and in private hands as at Hassendean, the owners wish to restore the structure.

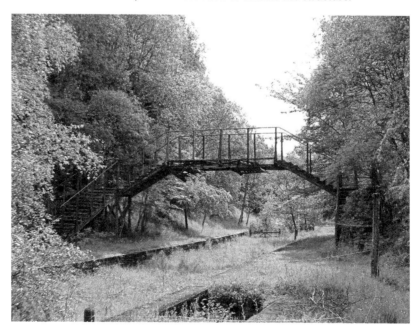

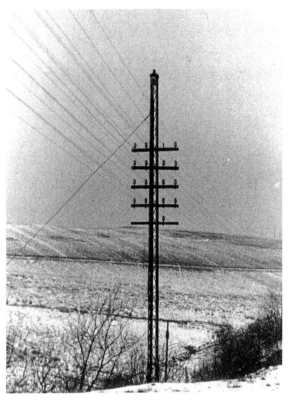

An unusual re use for a NBR lattice signal post. Due to signal re-siting, assumed to be to do with the Stobs Army Camp construction, this former down starting signal was taken into use as a telegraph route.

A remarkable surviving relic, it can still be seen here in 2006, standing quietly among the trees.

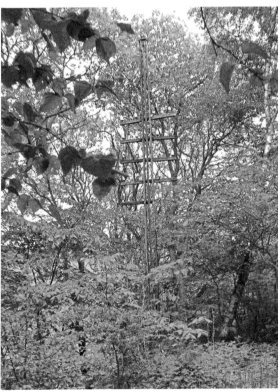

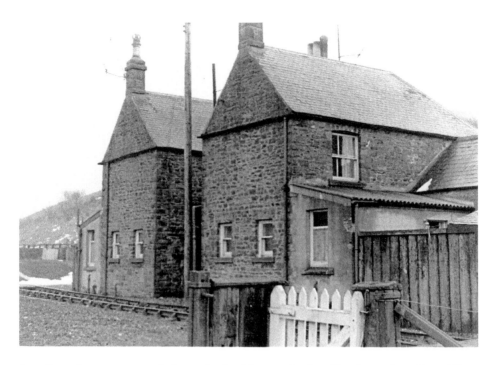

Seen from the entrance road, the station building at Shankend has been altered by infilling between the two gables and by the addition of extra windows.

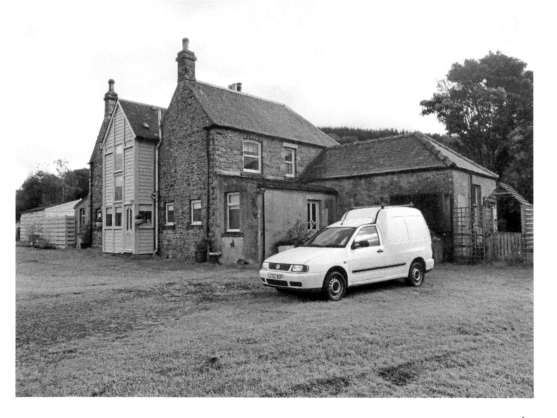

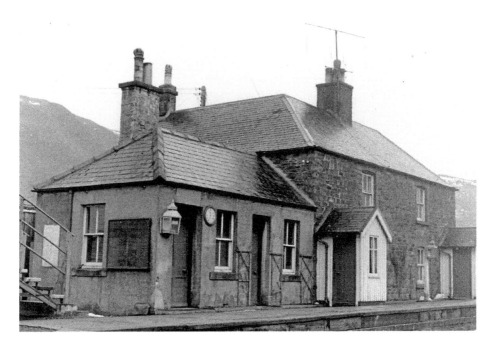

The platform side of the Shankend station building.

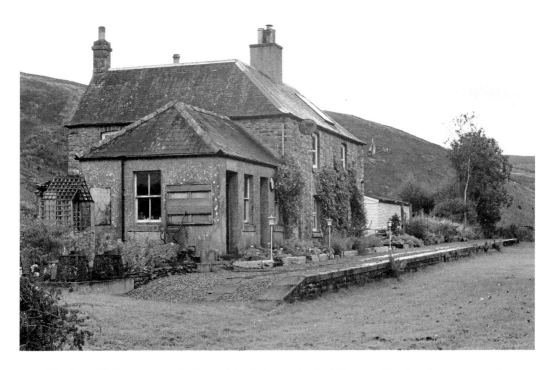

The beautifully restored platform side of the station buildings at Shankend is an example to all. The un-original storm porches have been removed but otherwise the view is similar to that from 1969 shown above, bar some minor changes such as the original lamps being removed and the re-positioning of the clock.

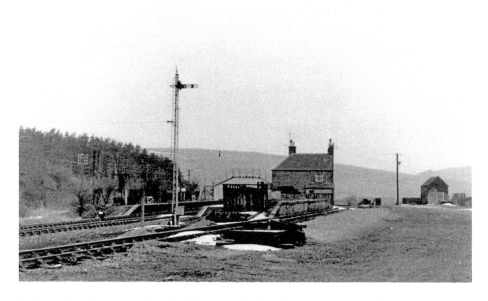

A view taken from near the signal box at Shankend in 1969, showing the station, station buildings, loading bay and the remaining siding.

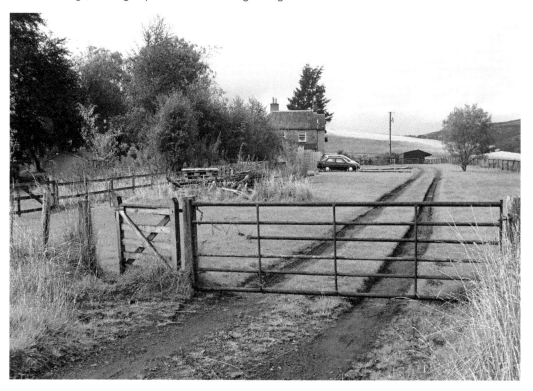

A similar view from 2012 shows the approach road to the signal box and the station building.

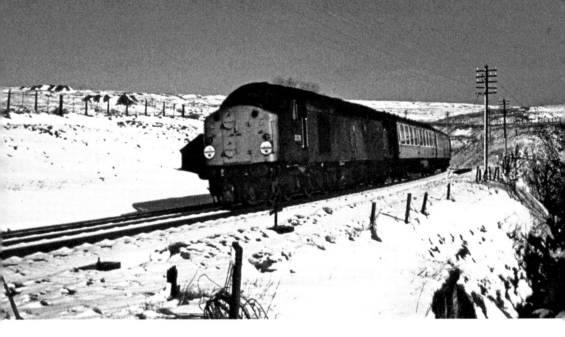

A blue Type 4 breasts the summit on a passenger turn. At 1,006 feet above sea level, Whitrope is the highest point on the line and is now home to the Waverley Route Heritage Association and their operational arm, the Border Union Railway Company Ltd.

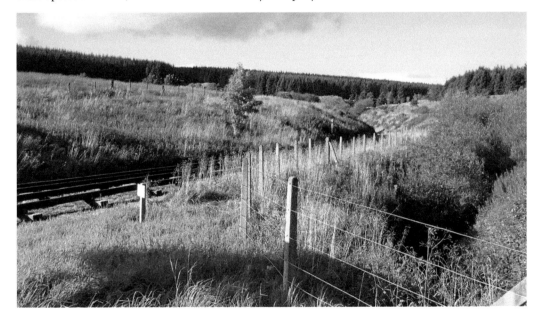

Created in 2001 with the primary aim of safeguarding structures and the route in general, this site has now developed into a heritage railway centre with driver experience turns and a museum to be enjoyed on site. This is the only such publically accessible location on the route to offer such an attraction in 2012.

This author would like to suggest to the viewer that the delights of Liddesdale be sampled. It is a fantastic natural resource in which to spend an afternoon, week or holiday, although I appreciate that I am somewhat biased in my views.

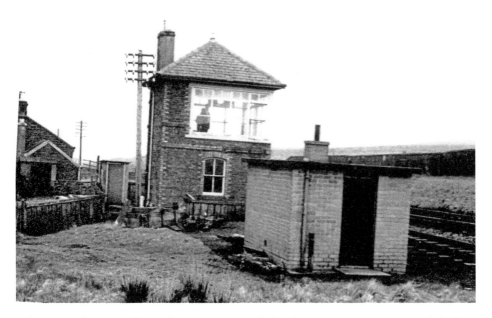

Whitrope Siding Signal Box, demonstrating well the elevation of the site. Beyond the box, it looks to all intents and purposes that the world is flat and that the end has just been reached.

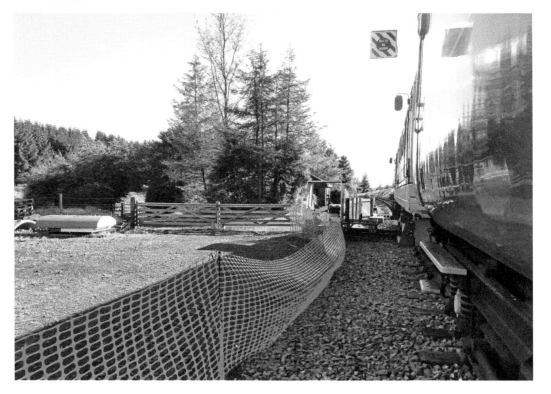

The signal box stood just behind the trees in rear of the gates. Some of the WRHA/BURC collection is on view here and the aforestation of the area is clearly evident.

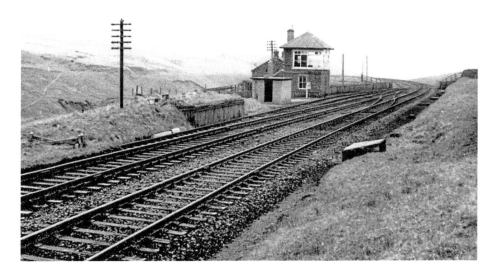

Again, the 'edge of the world' can be clearly seen here, along with the signal box, siding and loading dock. If the juxtaposition of the siding in relation to the running line looks a little suspect, it is due to the gradient of the main lines here, with the summit still being 200 yards behind the camera.

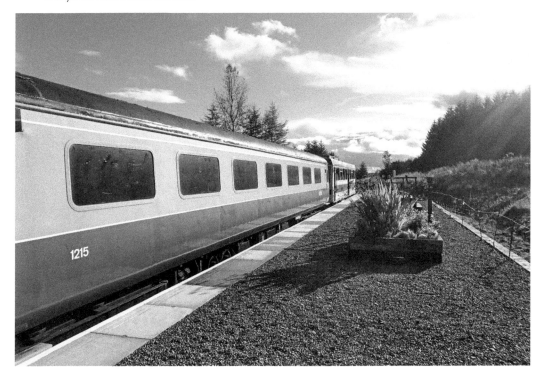

Railbus RB004, a Mk2 coach, a platform and well tended flowerbeds now adorn this scene. A true credit to the dedication of the volunteers, and I think it fundamental to stress this, who give all their time so freely and without hesitation.

A kind thank you also goes to Northumbria Rail, whose rolling stock is on loan and in view.

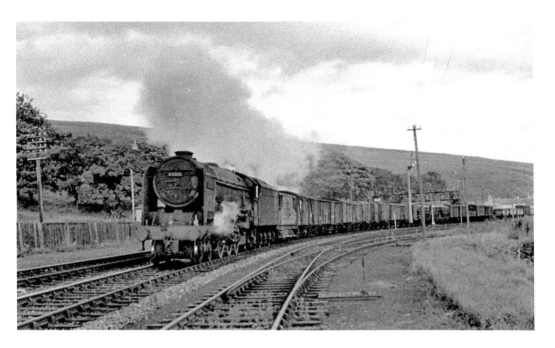

A2/3 60512, *Steady Aim*, lives up to its name as it pounds the bank through Riccarton, putting her fireman to 'useful service'. The climb would be over in 2¼ miles and a pleasurable 10½ mile drift down the other side would be afforded to the footplate crew, until they relieved a south-bound service at Hawick and it started all over again.

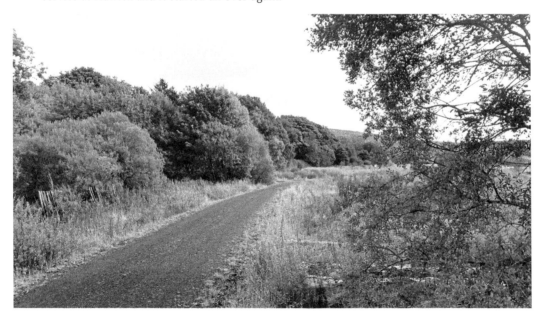

What remains of the sleeper deflection fence can be seen to the left in 2012 and a forestry haul road now occupies the former main line. Riccarton has, however, recently witnessed rail traffic once more: three times in 2012 alone, albeit carried on the back of a Reids transport low loader. A sight to behold in its own right for those who are aware of the nature of the local roads and the descent upon said delivery vehicles by the local rally drivers. You know who you are.

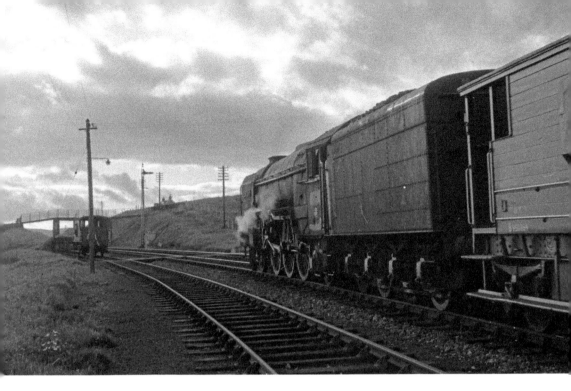

Steady Aim again here slogs past the photographer. Phaupknowe House can be seen above her and the headshunt for the once considerable siding complex contains a brakevan to the left.

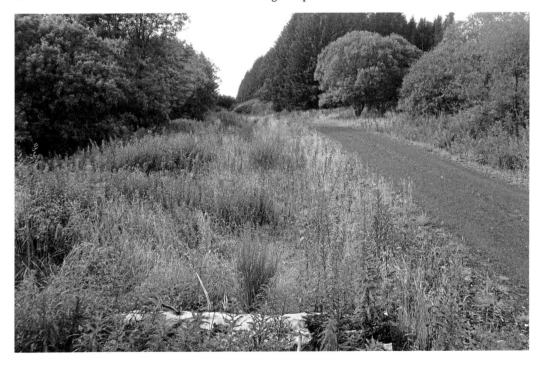

The forestry haul road continues into the depths of a now vast plantation. The wilds of this area of the Cheviots have now succumbed to the march of the Sitka spruce from the Kielder Forest.

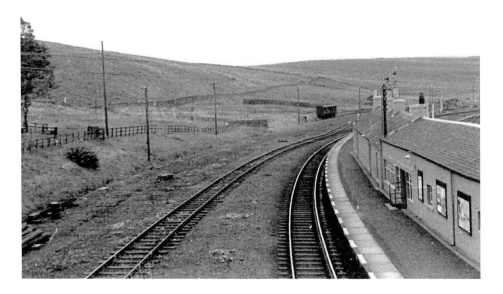

The view south from the station footbridge demonstrates well the desolate nature of Riccarton. Rationalisation of the sidings and loops had already been undertaken by the time of this 1966 study, with only a single siding of the original four loops remaining.

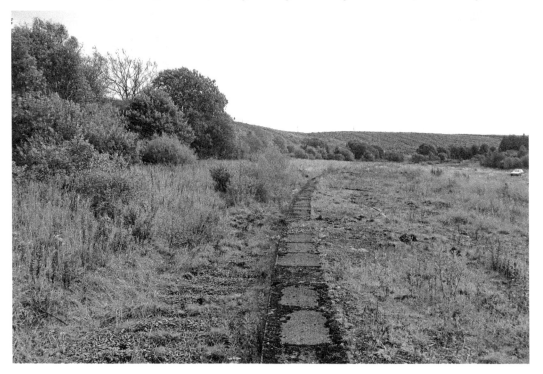

No true comparison can now be made, with the footbridge from which the historic shot was taken removed. A once thriving but remote community existed here and started to succumb to the march of progress with the closing of the Border Counties to passengers in 1956.

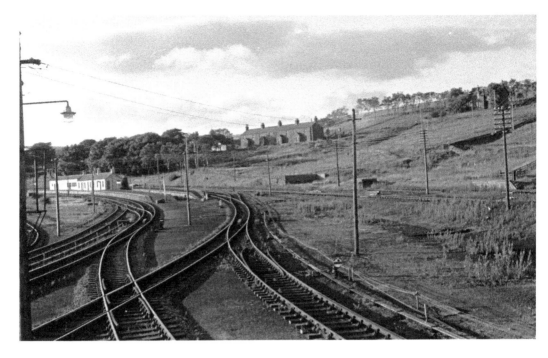

The reason Riccarton Junction was so named and the source of its activity. Running to the left is the main line to Carlisle, and to the right the Border Counties to Hexham. The original bay platform stands devoid of its tracks in this view. The south terrace can been seen on the hillside and the replacement shed, coaling stage and turntable stood to the right.

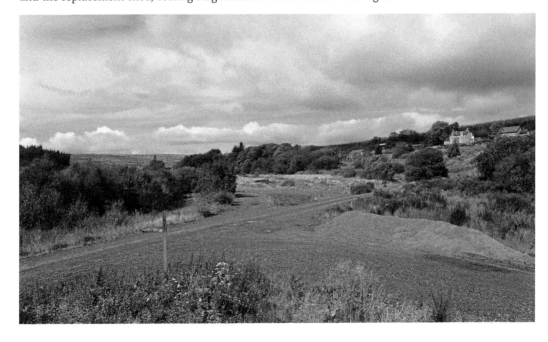

The school house standing resplendent on the fellside above links these photographs, along with the rather useful direction of forestry haul roads. The elevated contemporary study was achieved by standing on the signal box rubble and holding the camera aloft, no easy feat.

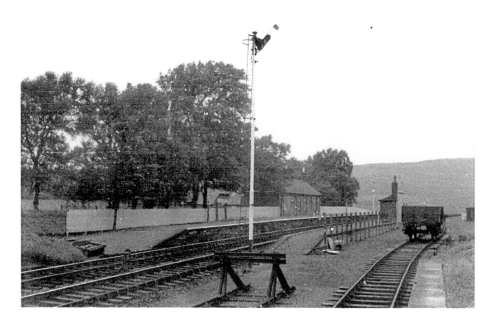

The station at Steele Road was another small rural provision. A hamlet of railwaymen's cottages grew up in the vicinity and on closure of the Border Counties line, a replacement bus was laid on from here to Bellingham which did not last long at all.

A funny little waiting room was provided on the up platform, as can be seen here to the left of the wagon in the yard.

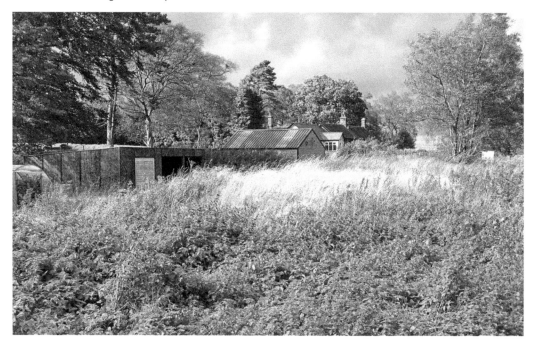

Today the former yard area to the south is overgrown and very wet. The main station buildings have been renovated and the area landscaped. Both platforms are still evident, although the track bed has been in filled and is home to a veg plot.

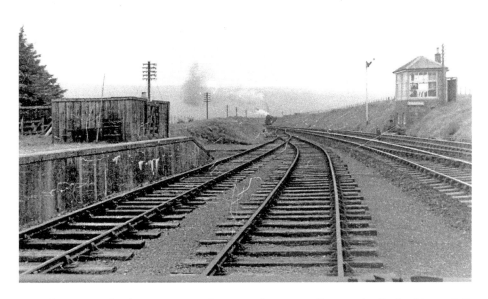

A V2 class engine battles its way out of time up the 1:75 gradient on the flank of Arton Fell. The signal box and yard throat are in evidence in this view south.

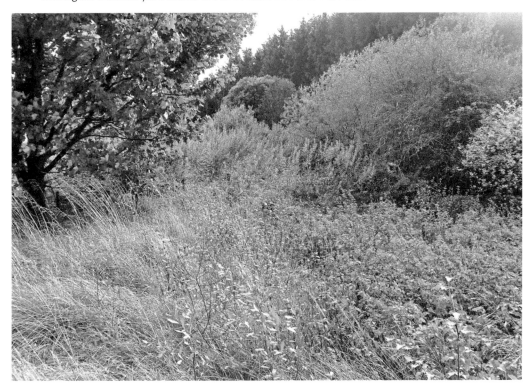

Barely recognisable today as the same location, only the imprint of the former formation and the retaining wall to the rear of the signal box survive, hidden among the vegetation.

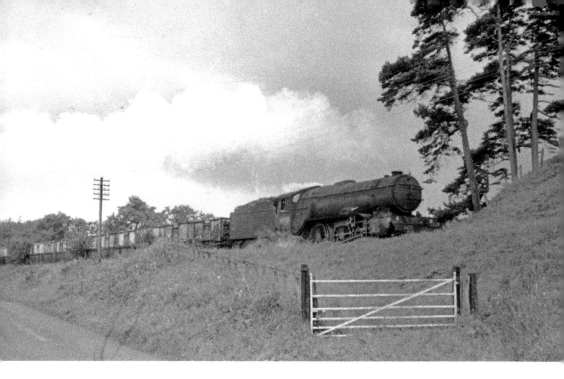

V2 Class 2-6-2 No. 60882 storms out of Newcastleton and on toward the Sandholm embankment, leading to Hermitage Viaduct and Steele Road, with northbound freight in 1962. Right through the 1950s and early 1960s, these locos were the mainstay of the freight and sometimes passenger services on the Waverley Route until dieselisation caused their withdrawl.

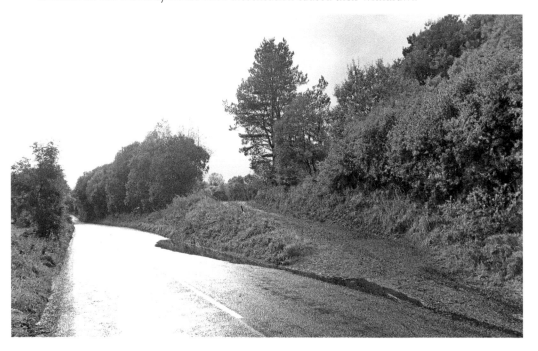

A similar view, again looking toward the Pathhead bridge and Newcastleton in 2012. The apparent narrowing of the road is an illusion caused by water on the road surface.

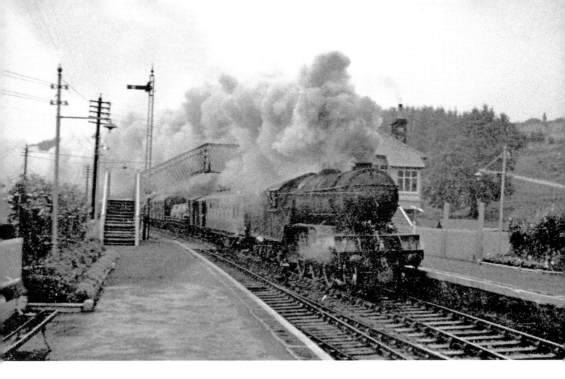

An unidentified A3 Class 4-6-2 storms through Newcastleton in attempt to charge the 'Whitrope Bank' which continued unbroken to Whitrope Summit. The Riccarton school coach can be observed next to the engine's tender after its sojourn in Carlisle.

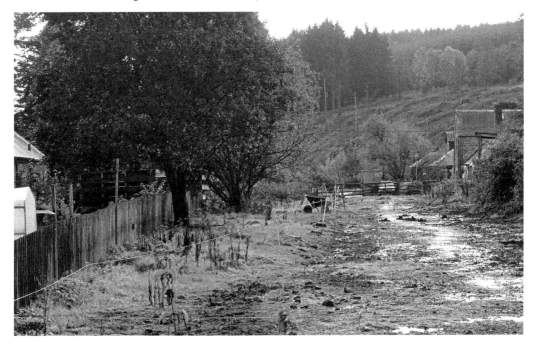

The station buildings, signal box, footbridge and platforms have been swept away in the orgy of destruction which followed closure, leaving only a muddy track where once stood a majestic railway.

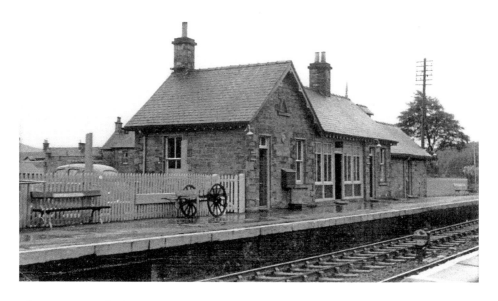

The neat station buildings in 1962, neatly maintained by generations of railwaymen until they were swept away in the name of economics. This was the up platform of the station.

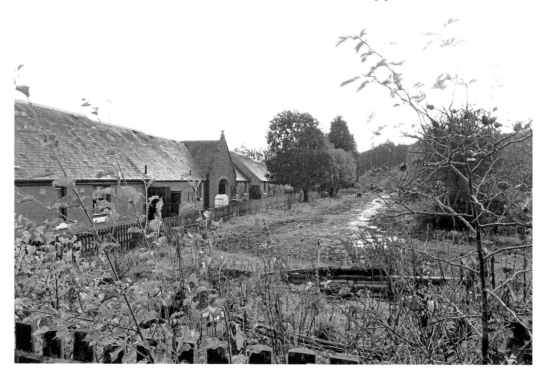

The casual observer could be excused for thinking that this had been the station building on the left but it is in fact of much newer provenance, having been built after the station was demolished in 1971.

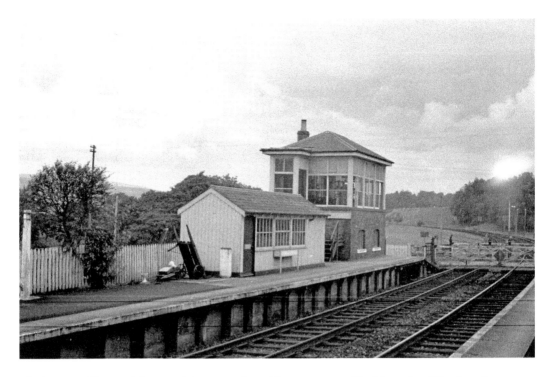

The fine signal box and down waiting room alongside are portrayed in this study of Kershopefoot. The line can be seen curving along the Liddel Valley floor beyond.

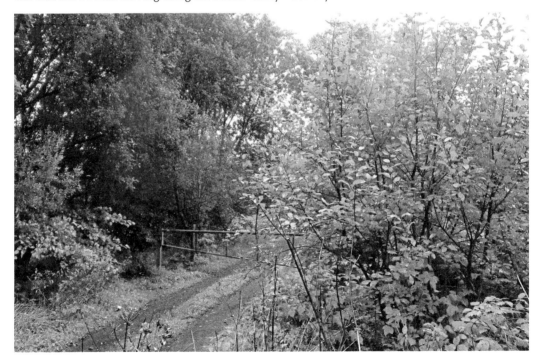

Trees now occupy the area as it returns to nature. The trackbed is used to access the forestry to the south at this location now.

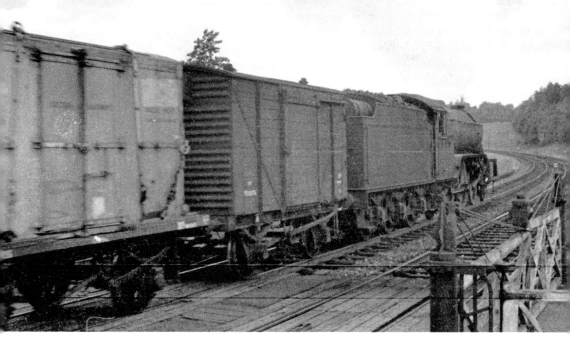

An unidentified V2 shatters the peace as it swings through the station on a Carlisle Canal Yard to Niddrie Yard freight in 1962.

This was the opportunity to pick up speed for the climb to Whitrope Summit. The route dropped from the summit at Nook to the south and ran on level or light gradients until the serious climb began at Path Head in Newcastleton to the north.

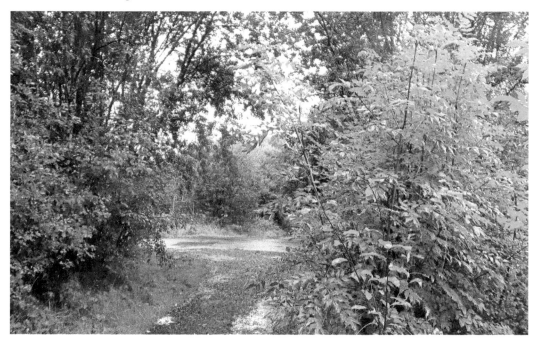

This tranquil valley is now an avenue of trees and no such engines are to be witnessed or heard here. The Reiver Trail now follows the formation along to Mangeton Tower, one of the Reiver Clans' seats, and onto Newcastleton. Although wet in parts, it is an easy and very pleasing walk.

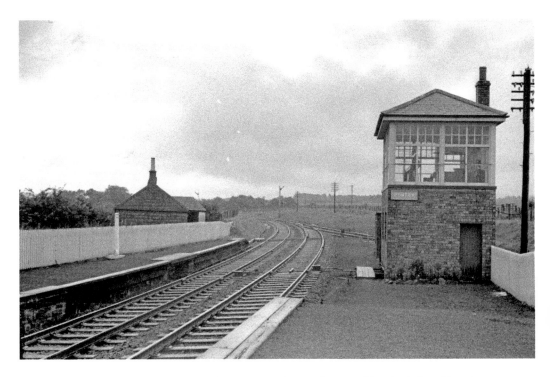

Looking south from Penton Station in the summer of 1968; the signal box had closed in February of that year.

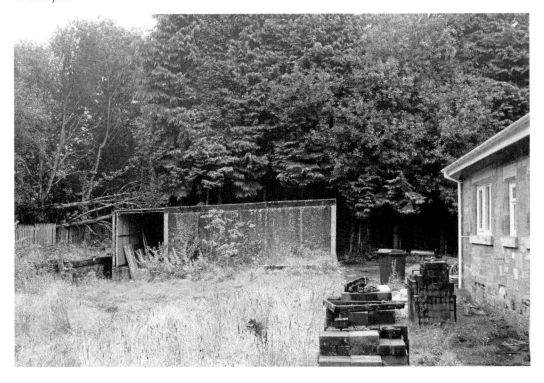

A substantial screen of trees blocks a similar view in 2012.

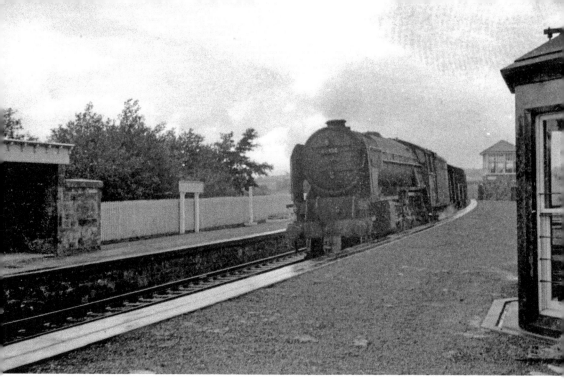

Peppercorn Class A2 No. 60530 *Sayajirao* hurries southward through Penton with a freight in 1965.

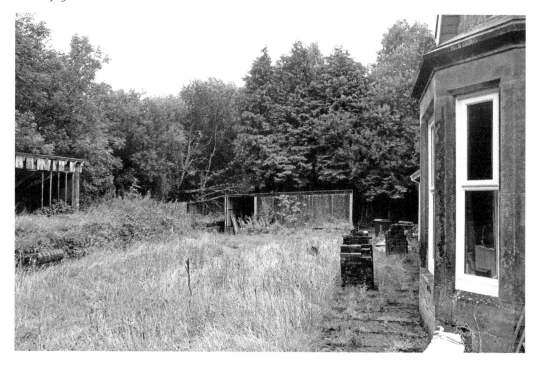

This was the same view in 2012; the track bed is now blocked with trees.

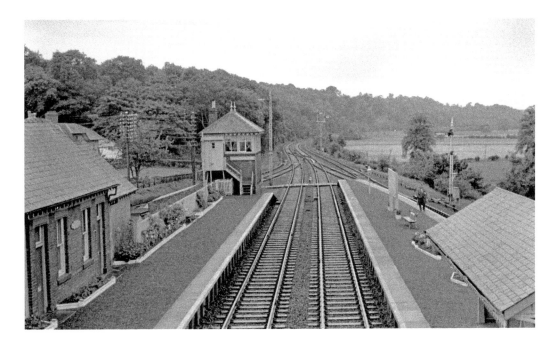

Riddings formed the junction for the 7-mile branch to Langholm via Canonbie, which was actually situated in Rowanburn. The station was really an interchange for this purpose although in practice the branch trains originated from Carlisle Citadel Station. The view south from the footbridge illustrates well the layout of the station, which is shown to be well tended.

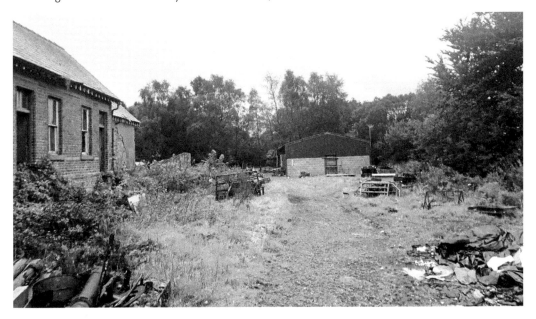

With the removal of passenger services to Langholm in 1965, the platforms were quickly swept away. The branch limped on for freight for another 2 years, finally closing in 1967, at which point Riddings ceased to be a junction.

The station buildings on the up platform were retained and still stand in 2012, but in poor condition; however, the signal box has been demolished.

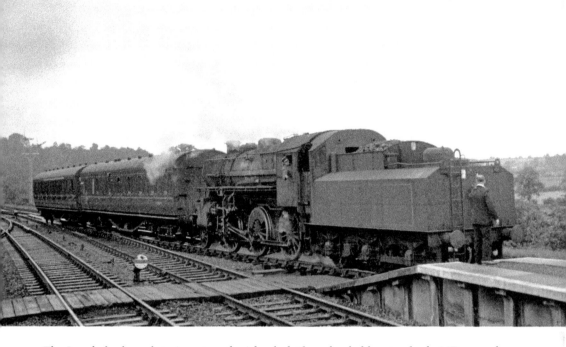

The Langholm branch train enters the island platform hauled by standard 4MT 43139, known affectionately by footplate crews as 'Jezebel'. The driver prepares to accept the branch token from the signalman at the platform end. This locomotive was a regular engine for this and the pick up freight duties of the branch.

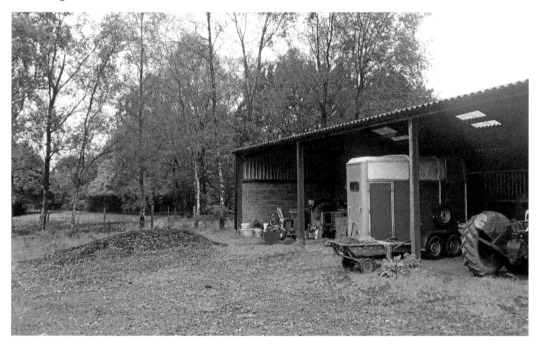

A new open-front agricultural building and a horses' paddock now occupy the junction main line and refuge site.

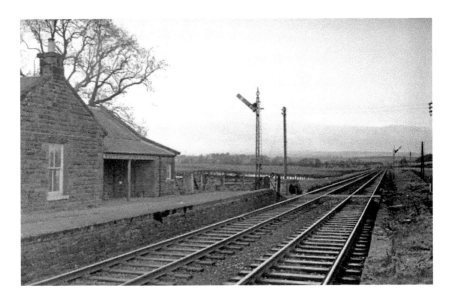

The view north through Scotch Dyke Station shows a long straight which would have allowed for fast running were it not for the curvature and associated speed restriction behind the camera.

The station opened before the full opening of the line south of Hawick in 1862, but was to close in 1949. The legend 'Speed and Comfort by Rail' was written on the main building's canopy and is still legible to this day. (R. B. McCartney Collection)

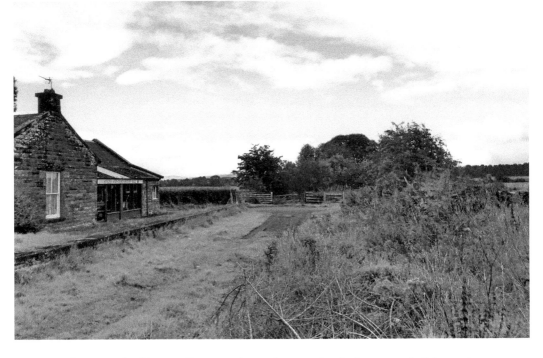

The station buildings still exist in domestic use and only the removal of the tracks and up platform and the growth of trees change the scene. The River Esk is crossed half a mile to the north and the formation runs along the wide valley floor.

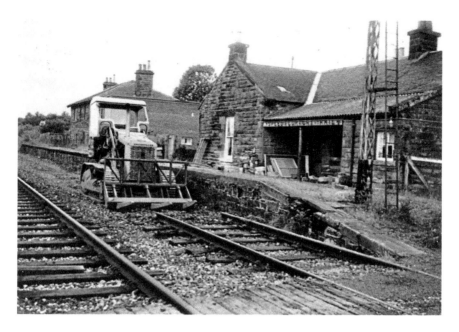

The main station building is shown here at track lifting in 1970/71 with the railway cottages beyond. (R. B. McCartney Collection)

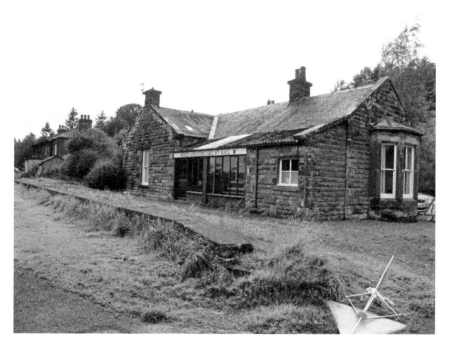

The obvious removal of the tracks and the very slight modification to the buildings are the differences between then and now. (R. B. McCartney)

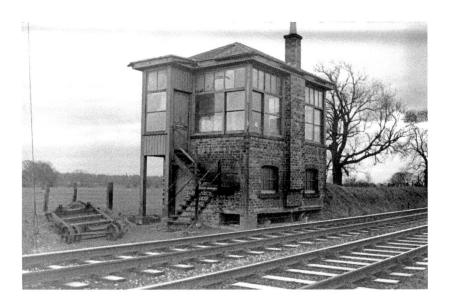

The signal box shown here was constructed to the north of Scotch Dyke Station and level crossing. This replaced an earlier box to the south, opposite the former yard. Although it was closed and replaced with a lever frame in 1954, the box stood well into the 1970s before succumbing to the bulldozer. (R. B. McCartney Collection)

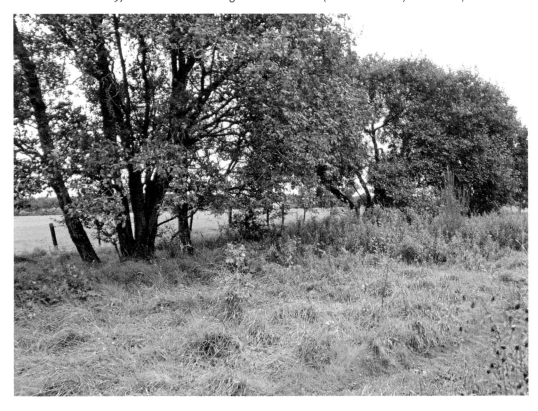

It is still possible to find evidence on the ground here today for the box's existence; some brick work and sections of guttering can found.

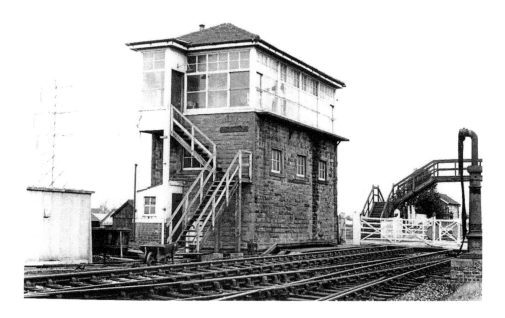

The imposing signal box stood guardian over the level crossing and Gretna branch junction. The branch to Gretna had a chequered history, being closed and then reopened due to demand before finally closing other than to serve the MoD site. It was again returned to use in 1963 for up arrivals to the new Kingmoor Marshalling Yard, north of Carlise.

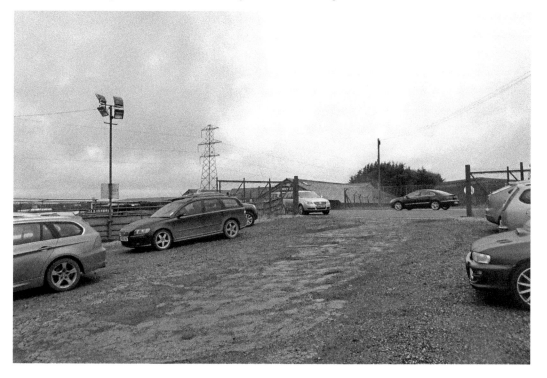

The whole area has been levelled and only the National Grid pylon serves as a point of comparison.

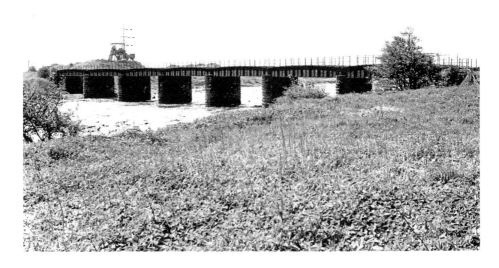

The River Esk was crossed immediately to the south of the Gretna junction on a seven-span plate girder viaduct. Sat on low masonry piers with cut waters to channel the fast-flowing Esk, the viaduct made for an imposing sight.

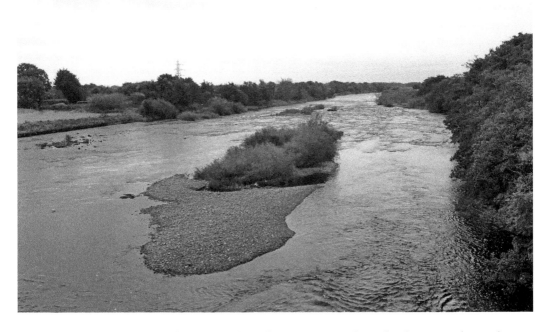

Removed with indignant haste, the Esk Viaduct is no more. The embankment on the south side of the river is identifiable by the row of trees.

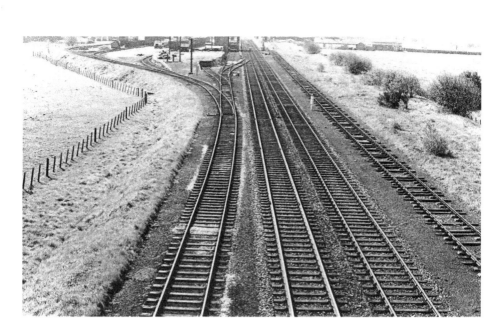

The length and size of the former yard can be seen here. Longtown Station and Yard were located right next to the livestock auction mart, which developed sizeable receipts figures for the railway.

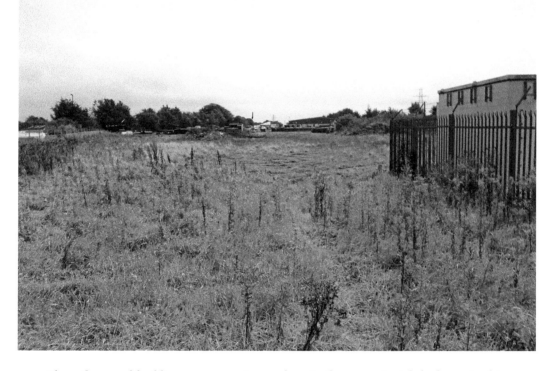

The railway and buildings were swept away here in the 1970s. A stub had remained in use from Kingmoor for MoD traffic as MoD Longtown and Smalmstown could only be accessed from this direction until Mossband Junction on the West Coast Main Line was re-signalled to accept north-bound traffic on to the branch.

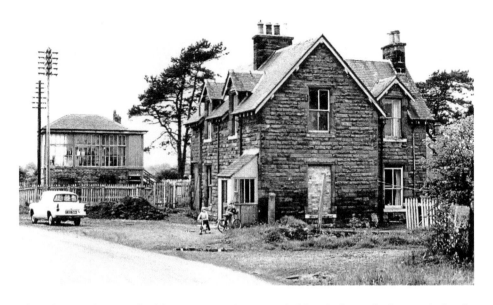

The substantial station building at Lyneside was probably a little on the large side for the modest passenger numbers that came from the hamlet of West Linton, which it was built to serve. The station was closed by the LNER in 1929 and passed into private ownership. The signal box continued in its role until final closure in 1969.

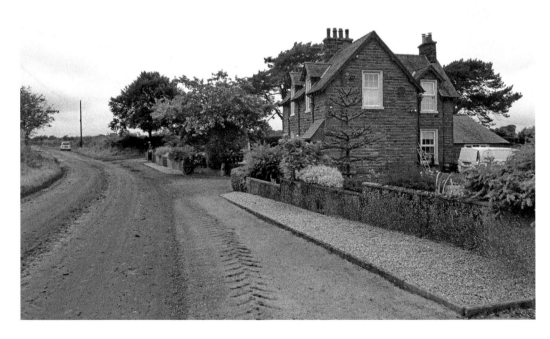

The station building remains largely unaltered to this day. The base of the signal box is used as garden storage to tend the well manicured gardens which now occupy the formation.

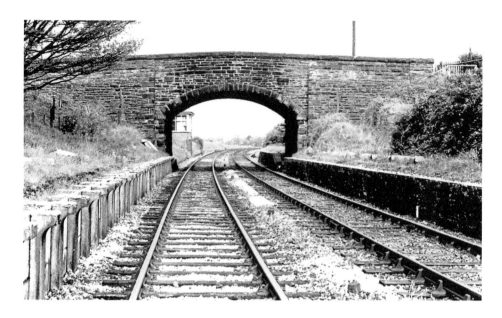

Harker is a tale of two stations. The first had opened with the line but closed in 1929 as an economy measure. Reopened again during the war to serve the munitions factories, it was retained throughout for workers' traffic. The new station is well illustrated here, to the south side of the former site, through the bridge.

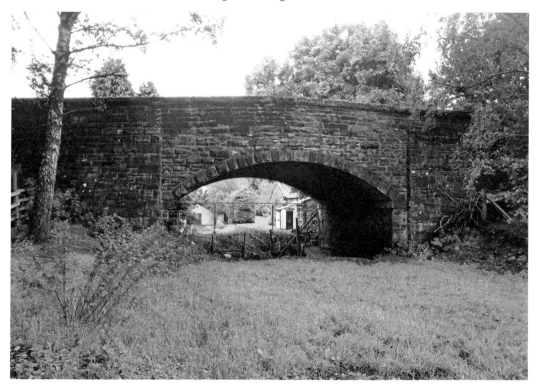

The area of the platforms is now back filled but they are still there and could be seen until 2010. The stub of the first station's up platform can be seen under the bridge.

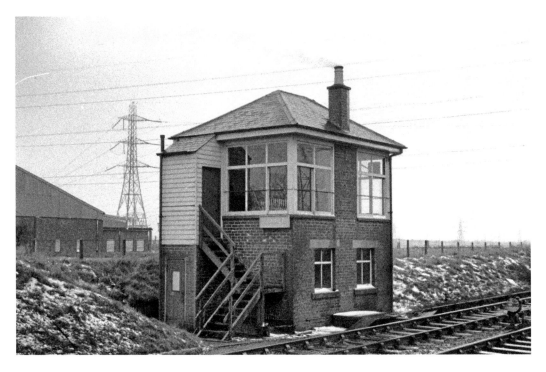

Harker Signal Box was retained following the station closure for the sidings and block post. It finally closed in 1966.

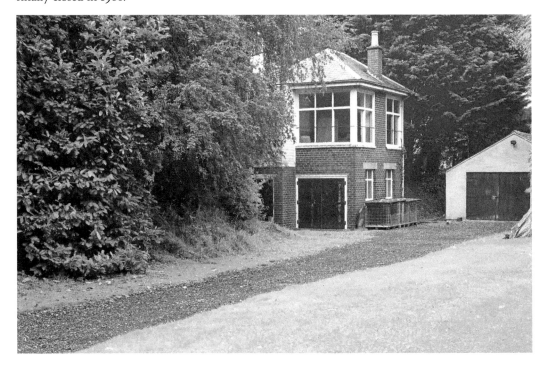

The box was taken over, along with the track bed, by the station's owner after track lifting and has survived to this date in use as a very grand garden shed and summer house.

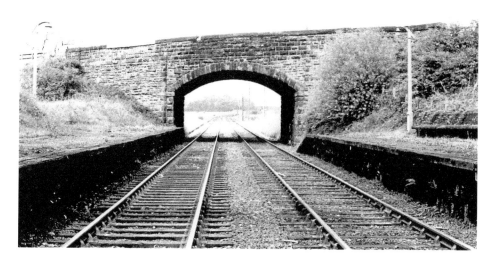

Parkhouse Halt was not an advertised station and was constructed to serve the works traffic for the neighbouring RAF MU14 complex. The proximity to Harker can be seen here. The railway horizon through the bridge's span is the location of the Harker platforms.

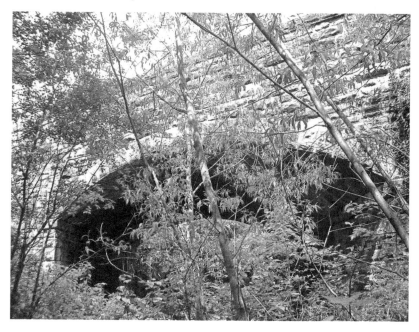

This location is now very overgrown but Bridge 260, which carried the old A74 Glasgow road over the site, still stands and can be seen from the M6/M74 motorway which runs behind the bridge.

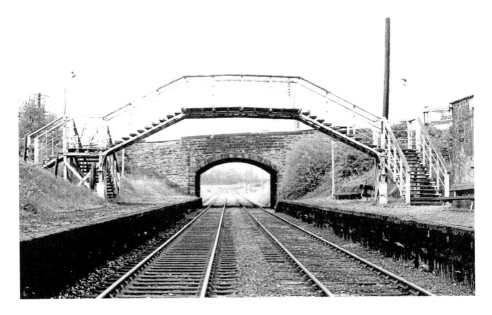

The sparse, utilitarian nature of the halt is clearly evident. Waiting rooms were provided for shelter, along with the foot bridge to cross the line, as seen, but no main buildings existed.

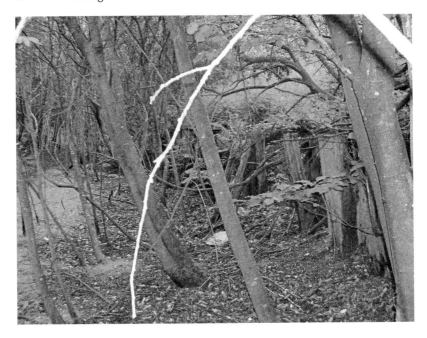

No true contemporary shot is possible here due to the vastly overgrown nature of the site. It is also incredibly dark below the dense canopy, but it is possible to make out the quietly rotting remains of the up platform. Several concrete lamp standards still remain in among the trees.

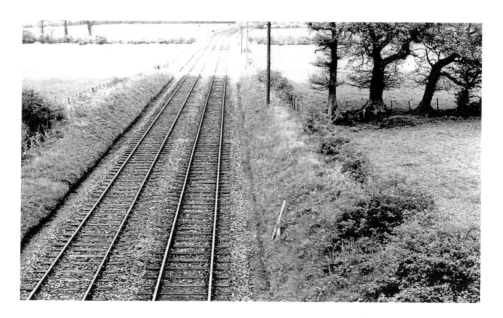

The view north from the A74 overbridge. The line was constructed over very gentle gradients and curves as it crossed the low flat lands between here and Longtown and speeds up to 70mph could be experienced, in sharp contrast to the heavy slogs over the summits.

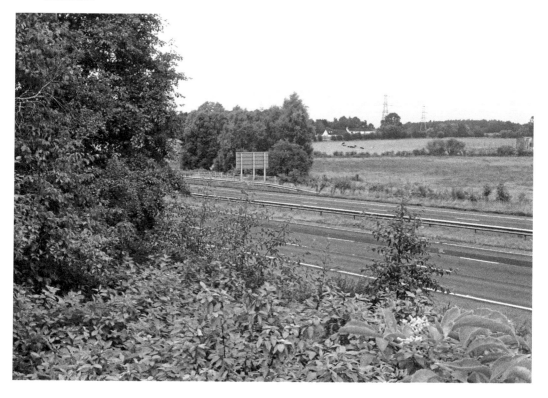

Today the motorway bisects the formation, as the line is identified by the tree growth over the trackbed.

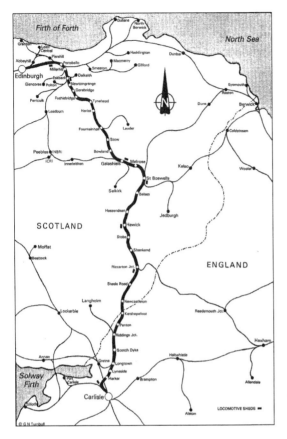

A map showing the Waverley Route from Edinburgh to Carlisle. (G. N. Turnbull and the WRHA Archive)

Acknowledgements

The authors wish to exspress their thanks and gratitude to the following people for their assistance and encouragement.

Bruce McCartney for photographic provision, encouragement and assistance; Jane and Paul Langley, Andrew and Sarah MacIntosh, Janet and Lawson Short and Valerie Collins for assistance with proof reading.

Marcus Day, Tomasz Milkowski, Dave Smith, Tony 'Colin McCrea' Graham and Gary Ormiston for assistance with transport.

A further thank you must go to Heather Park, Louis Archard, the JDP group of Longtown and to all the private owners who have been so kind and tolerating during our visits.

A most sincere thank you to all.

Unless otherwise stated, modern images have been taken by Iain MacIntosh and old images are from the Roy G. Perkins Collection.

Roy G. Perkins and Iain MacIntosh.